dharma mind worldly mind

DAVID SMITH

dharma mind
worldly mind

A Buddhist Handbook on
Complete Meditation

ALOKA PUBLICATIONS

Published by
Aloka Publications
email: information@dharmamind.net
web: www.dharmamind.net

Printed and bound by Antony Rowe Ltd., Eastbourne
Design Dhammarati

British Library Cataloguing in Publications Data:
A catalogue record of this book is available from the British Library

ISBN 0 9542475 0 7

Contents

Acknowledgements

I would like to express my gratitude to both Jnanasiddhi and Shantavira for their efforts with their editorial skills in helping put this book together, and to Vessantara who helped with the editing also but in addition gave me the support throughout that has made it possible for my manuscript to finally be published. And my gratitude goes also to Mike Leonard for creating the website that is important in making this work known.

Dharma Mind Worldly Mind

Dharma Mind
'Mind' is used as the translation of the Pali and Sanskrit word Citta. Citta means both the mind that is the thinking faculty in the head, but more especially, mind that is the intuitive, emotional 'heart' of our being, and located in our body. It is here 'beyond the thinking mind' in the body that the Dharma Mind is to be nurtured, for it is here that Truth waits to be discovered. The thinking mind has its part to play in the discovering of the Dharma, but is to be used only as a skilful means to help sift and understand the verbal and written Dharma that we all take in on our spiritual pilgrimage of discovery.

Worldly Mind
I use this term to denote our normal everyday mind and state of being that is goal-oriented and saturated in ego and self-interest. This ego and self-interest, in its conceit, turns away from the Citta as a whole thus making it impossible for it ever to know the Truth.

Introduction

One of the great joys I experienced shortly after the publication of my book *A Record of Awakening* was engagement in the question-and-answer sessions at various Buddhist centres around the British Isles that followed the launch.

This first book was an attempt to express the deep spiritual understanding that arose in me in Sri Lanka in 1981, though I only wrote the first draft some eight years later, in 1989, while living in London. On completion, I put the draft in my desk drawer and forgot about it for quite some years. One day, however, just out of curiosity, I searched it out and read it over again, and I was surprised how much I liked what I had written. In the intervening years I had learned how to use a computer and gained experience in word-processing so I decided to clean up my rather poor first draft and improve the general presentation. This took some time but eventually I had a presentable copy, which I then had ambitions to get published.

The preface, written by the founder of the Friends of the Western Buddhist Order, Urgyen Sangharakshita, picks up the story of how it was finally published by Windhorse Publications in November 1999. For me this was quite an achievement; to write a manuscript that finally reached publication was something beyond my dreams. Publishing a book didn't somehow seem to fit the sort of upbringing I had – a very ordinary working class background in Oxford, England. I am the son of a car worker, and at the age of 25 I decided to travel the world just for the sake of it. It was while leading a quite hedonistic existence in Sydney, Australia, that I found Buddhism – through books. Reading the Dharma – the teaching of the Buddha – transformed my whole life, and the reason for living it.

I returned to my native England to seek out a Zen teacher, as this was the form of Buddhism that interested me most at the time. I trained with that teacher for nearly six years before becoming a Theravada monk in Sri Lanka. It is my experiences there in the subtropics that are the main focus of the first book. After three years in Sri Lanka I disrobed and returned to the UK, where, despite retaining my Theravada links in this country, I have on the whole been practising on my own ever since. The major change since the launch of that book has been the opportunity to transmit some of my understanding of the Dharma to fellow practitioners through Dharma groups that I lead.

At the book launches I was struck very strongly by the interest and enthusiasm shown by the audience in the book itself, but also by their enthusiasm and desire for knowledge about how to practise the Buddha's Path. So whilst there were a few predictable questions on metaphysics, and a few even more predictable questions expressing curiosity about my own practice, the great majority of queries were about their own practice: how they should approach it and how they should deal with the difficulties they encountered.

It has been this experience above all else that has motivated me to put together this second book. I consider it to be really a continuation from the first publication, committing to paper the answers to most of the questions I was asked at the book launches. It also allows me to air several questions put to me during the many personal meetings I've had, and from the numerous letters and emails I have received following the book's publication. I have also included one or two extra pointers and suggestions which the reader may find useful.

I hope you will discover whilst reading that this really isn't a book of lists and formulas but rather an expression of a living experience. Because of this flavour you will often come across words that try to convey that living experience – which is an emotional one. We are sensitive, warm-blooded mammals, and our feelings and emotions are the predominant experience of our life. Throughout the book you will come across expressions such as negative and positive emotions, and words such as feelings, outflows, passions, etc. All these words point to the differing intensity of our emotional experience. I hope all these words are self-explanatory, but just a note on the word 'passion'. It is used in this book to express a more intense experience than the expression 'negative emotion' can convey. It describes those times when we are really caught up in our emotions and carried away by an experience of gripping intensity – falling into an old familiar habit that we have little or no control over. The taming of the passions is the most important part of practice.

I have tried to make my responses and reflections to Dharma questions as short and to the point as possible, so that the reader can take them in and reflect on them without having to wade through lots of background and incidental information. However, at some points in the text I couldn't help drawing things out more than I would have wished, just because I found that I needed to construct a framework so that the point being made could be seen more clearly and in context. I am presuming, however, that the reader has at least some basic knowledge of the principles of Buddhism. It is my hope that those who are practising the bodhisattva path of the mahayana (the 'great vehicle' of Buddhism) will use this book, especially at those times when we discover we are lost and confused and when the inevitable difficulties arise and we struggle to know what is happening to us and what to do next?

Special Mind

Those of us who practise the Dharma are often in the position of reading books or listening to talks so that our knowledge has a chance to grow and deepen. But do we really know how to open to the Dharma during these times? It does take a special type of mind, not the one we would normally employ while accumulating more worldly knowledge. Our usual way of absorbing knowledge and trying to understand something is accompanied by a process of sifting thoughts and notions that are based on established assumptions and knowledge that we already have. The mind is therefore engaged in thinking and absorbing at the same time. The mind that we use to absorb the Dharma should be quite different.

When listening to the Dharma it is best to try to keep your mind empty of thoughts and judgements, not to engage with them and get caught up in them. The correct way is to be like an empty vessel. Just open and let the Dharma pour in, let it pour into your being, into your heart. Don't stop it with thoughts, don't scrutinize it and play it off with what you already know – for you cannot do this and be fully alive and receptive to the subtleties that are always inherent in the Dharma. The wholeness of the message may well be missed. So empty the mind whilst reading this book. Indeed, see it as an opportunity for meditation, where you are clearing the mind of thoughts and obstructions, and stay concentrated on the Dharma in this book.

The Dharma has two quite contradictory characteristics: it is immensely powerful yet, paradoxically, very
fragile. It is powerful because it is capable of sweeping
the world away with a stroke. Yet unless you create the
conditions of openness and stillness, and allow it to enter
you at times of learning, without the impediment of
thoughts and views, it will not manifest. Just a thought
that comes when you are supposed to be open, just a
wrong view that may arise at this time, just a moment's
inattention while you are supposed to be attentive, is
enough to prevent its entry, and it is deflected, gone, and
will remain so until you create the correct conditions
again.

While contemplating these two apparently contradictory characteristics, consider a third, and that is the very
subtle nature of the Dharma. This is why we have to
approach Dharma input with this special mind. By allowing it to enter without obstructions we are allowing it to
penetrate deeply into our heart and saturate our entire
being.

Do not worry about suspending your thoughts and
opinions in this way; the Dharma you have taken in will
not be lost, so there is no need to chase after it. If you
have listened to a talk on Dharma, with your hands
joined, bow your head at the end in gratitude to both the
speaker and to the Dharma, then go to a quiet place and
muse over what you have heard. Try not to just think
about it. If you can't remember all that has been said, you
may indeed have forgotten most of it. Don't worry – it is

there, deep within, and it will always be there, waiting to arise when the conditions are ripe. But if you take yourself off, and are still and open, it will likely arise by itself to the surface of your mind for you to ponder and comprehend.

While the Dharma that you have opened up to may still only be a concept, a word, a sound, it is still able to have a profound effect on you if it is pondered quietly and deeply. What was once just a concept can commune and connect with that which is beyond concepts, and genuine insight can arise, insight that can become a part of your reality, that has strength for you to draw on in your life. All this is possible because you have learned to listen with a special mind.

After reading this book you can ponder or return to parts of it, or put it to one side, if you choose, but why not try to bring into being that special mind while you take in the words you are about to read? Who knows where they may lead?

The Basics of Practice

Introduction

In order to be as precise and as direct as possible in the body of this book, I would like to take the opportunity here to create a background to the practice. Most of you reading this will already be practising in a similar way – engaging in this practice that will hopefully one day, as a result of all our efforts, take you beyond the endless cycle of dukkha that we clearly experience in our life and want very much to put an end to.

Those of us who are attracted to Buddhism and its practices have experienced the unsatisfactoriness or suffering of life (dukkha) at least to the extent that we responded when we came in contact with the Dharma. So now, at the very least, we begin to understand why life is this way. We see, and may have seen before we even found Buddhism that the basis of dukkha has very much to do with our self or ego, with its perpetual preoccupation with self interest and its desire to control so many experiences in our life. Seeing those two facts within ourselves means we have already reflected on the first two of the four noble truths – the truth of suffering and the cause of suffering, the third truth being that there is a way out of suffering and the fourth being the way of practice. These four truths are the very heart of the Buddha's teaching and are found in all schools of Buddhism, however they may be dressed up or disguised.

The great attraction, when I first came across Buddhism was not so much the affirmation of the first two truths. What attracted me was that it then went on to offer me the third truth – that proclaimed there was a way out of this dilemma, which I had thought forever entrapped me. Discovering it was possible to end my woes made me give up my fun life in Australia all those years ago and return to my home country. In England I knew there were Dharma teachers who could teach me how to experience the fourth and last noble truth – the wonderful wisdom and practice of the eightfold path. This was the practice that I intended to take hold of and nurture with all my determination, in order to get me off this wheel of eternal becoming.

That brings us to the basics of the complete practice of the Buddha-Dharma. In order for there to be the change in ourselves that most of us very much desire, we need to understand the central and most important teaching of the Buddha – the eightfold path. Change will only really be possible in a deep and meaningful way when we are prepared to learn to cultivate the whole of this Path. In this section the Path is outlined so as to introduce it in its completeness. And whilst many may find the practice of the whole Path difficult, we must nevertheless realize that one day we will have to make that effort to round off and complete our practice of the Path.

This opening section also deals with going for refuge, which is another crucial element in change. Going for refuge is less tangible in many ways than the steps of the eightfold path, and can therefore be more difficult to cultivate, but it is crucial in that it completes the wholeness of practice which is our way forward into the great mystery of life – and therefore needs attention. Going for refuge possesses the indispensable quality of faith, which is the essential ingredient on our deepening spiritual journey. It could be said that going for refuge cradles and supports the eightfold path.

The third part of this section is an outline of the bodhisattva and how the spirit of this being is also an integral part of the complete practice. The bodhisattva, too, is cradled by going for refuge, so the essence of the bodhisattva practice cannot really be successfully formulated in the usual way because in this interpretation it is much more to do with the spirit of practice rather than any formula or concept. The spirit is one of openness and inclusivity of the whole of life without the discrimination of picking and choosing as to what you want your practice to include.

In order to make it clear what the Path is, we have to resort to this kind of breakdown – but it isn't so easy to see these different parts when there is commitment to a wholehearted practice. Commitment is the ingredient that unites and bonds these apparent differences, so while it is essential to understand the parts, unless they are brought together through commitment, the Path of liberation will always remain in the realms of theories and dreams.

The Eightfold Path

The eightfold path, consisting of right view, right resolve, right speech, right action, right livelihood, right effort, right concentration, and right mindfulness, is the way forward with practice. This path can be reduced to the more graspable threefold way of sila, samadhi, and prajna. Sila translates as ethics or conduct, samadhi as mindfulness and concentration, and prajna as wisdom – wisdom that has myriad levels but that eventually leads to 'knowing the way things really are'.

The practice of the eightfold path is often taught as something that is to be cultivated in a linear fashion. This is true to an extent – in that we have to learn to identify the three limbs (as the threefold way is often described) and give them individual attention. Ethics is considered to be primary; and so we have initially to cultivate our general behaviour through words, action, and how we make our living. Secondly we cultivate our ability to concentrate and be mindful primarily through meditation. Thirdly, we go on to develop our understanding of the Dharma, whether by reading, listening to other, or slowly beginning to understand ourselves. But as we are putting this convenient 'theory' into practice we soon discover that it is much more of an actual living process and can't always be approached in this convenient linear way.

It is hard to imagine that anyone with the self-awareness and sensitivity to at least be alive to their unsatisfactory human condition, and who seeks out Buddhism and its practices, will not have met the basic requirements of the three limbs of the threefold path: the sensitivity would lead them to an acceptable degree of behaviour which becomes the foundation of their practice of ethics; the self awareness indicates an ability, to some extent, to de-clutch from being caught and blinded and totally carried away by the turmoil of the coarse mind, which in turn indicates a degree of concentration thus fulfilling the basic requirement to practise the second limb; and the fact that they want to change their human condition indicates that they have reflected, probably to quite a lot on themselves, thus fulfilling the basic requirement to practise the third limb of wisdom.

We can see how, within normal everyday activity experienced even by the newly-born practitioner, the whole of the eightfold path is actually being practised. Whilst engaging in our daily life, we learn to hold on to and contain those familiar habitual outflows of words or actions driven by the emotions and passions, and that cause so many of our problems. We try our best to act and function as humanly as possible. By doing this we are practising sila. Because in the process of this containment we will be always restraining ourselves from being carried away by habits – and learning to stay centred within – we will be practising samadhi. And within that contained and concentrated state we will quite naturally become more and more familiar with ourselves and gain some understanding of why we are caught by these seemingly uncontrollable habits – the limb of wisdom. In this way, it is hard to imagine that anyone taking up Dharma practice hasn't actually already began to practise the Path. Indeed, a Zen master once said that self-awareness and the desire for release and change was enlightenment already.

So perhaps at first we focus on one of the limbs, then another, and then the third. Then we may bring one combination together, then another, then maybe one more combination. Then we cultivate all three limbs together. Sometimes we lose that final threefold combination and fall back into a two-way combination. Then sometimes we lose even that, and go back to just cultivating one limb. It doesn't matter, this to and fro, two steps forward and one step back. We keep mindfully endeavouring to bring all three limbs together. Slowly, slowly we become able to maintain a threefold practice until those three limbs are steady and consistent and harmonize with each other more and more.

In time this harmonizing becomes so balanced that we can actually see one limb in another limb, then another, then maybe yet another. Eventually we can see all three limbs in each limb – all perfectly balanced and in harmony with each other, until they merge and truly become just the one. When this state is realized, perfection of practice has been reached and the ultimate balance of the middle way (the true definition of the fourth noble truth, which is detailed later) attained. When that state of perfect balance – between the pull of opposites that characterize our mind and emotions – has reached perfection, there arises a seeing into the nature of mind that makes your entire consciousness, and the whole world, vanish, allowing awakening to be realized.

This is the path that we practise, whether we see it in those traditional terms or whether we use other concepts from less traditional schools, such as Zen, to pursue it. But the pursuit of the eightfold path has a very important extra feature to consider, for without it the realization of the middle way will be impossible, and that is the understanding and nurturing of going for refuge to the three jewels.

The Three Jewels
The three jewels are the Buddha, the Dharma, and the Sangha, and understanding the concept of going for refuge to these three jewels is absolutely crucial to the nurturing of true Dharma practice. It is the ongoing refinement of going for refuge over the years of practice that will be the framework, support, inspiration, and guide to the realization of ultimate truth.

This most basic of Buddhist principles – of going for refuge to the three jewels – is valid throughout Buddhism and accompanies almost every ritual that takes place. It is said that it is going for refuge that makes one a Buddhist, and signifies a commitment to the practice, so this ritual should be of deep importance and significance. But precisely because it is declared so regularly, the reflection on that importance and significance runs the danger of being neglected or even forgotten altogether, which is very unfortunate.

To take refuge in the Buddha, Dharma, and Sangha is of the utmost importance – and should be seen to be so – to serious Buddhists, those who consider themselves to be true and complete practitioners of the Way. When we take our commitment to the three jewels not just into our head but into our total being it becomes alive, it becomes the environment that the eightfold path is nurtured and cultivated in. We reaffirm this commitment continually by reflecting on the three jewels, and it is through this commitment that we gather the inner strength that is essential to walk the Way. When we have this commitment we have all the ingredients we need to change our life.

I followed Zen for nearly six years before leaving England to become a Theravada novice monk in Sri Lanka. One of the main characteristics of Zen is that it likes to describe itself as outside the scriptural teachings, a characteristic that makes many outside that school question its authenticity. It does not concern itself with the usual concepts of the more traditional approach. Going for refuge to the three jewels is not expressed in the usual way, but has its equivalent: the four great bodhisattva vows. These four vows can be presented in various ways but this interpretation is the one that I have always carried within myself.

> Innumerable are sentient beings, I vow to save them all.
> Inexhaustible are the passions, I vow to transform them all.
> Immeasurable are the Dharma teachings, I vow to
>   learn them all.
> Infinite is the Buddha-Truth, I vow to attain it.

I recited these regularly with the group that I practised with, and took them very much to heart and always saw them as central to my practice.

My first encounter with the more traditional version of the refuges took place in Sri Lanka at the time I was learning my ordination ceremony. There is very little taught about the importance of the refuges these days, so for me, at first, it was just part of the ritual. Even though I was about to partake of the more traditional version of commitment to Buddhism and its practice, I retained a great affinity with the bodhisattva vows I had recited for all those years.

Whilst contemplating the refuges I discovered that after my years of Zen practice I tended not to view the Buddha, Dharma, and Sangha in the way I would if I had begun my practice in the Theravada tradition. For me, the refuges had gone beyond the conventional, dualistic way of looking at them, into something deeper. Now the Buddha, Dharma, and Sangha were seen as something that was a part of me rather than something external.

In addition, I did not always find it easy to pull apart the Buddha and the Dharma – as they were now becoming one. The Buddha was not seen as only our historical founder, but as the wonder and mystery of life itself, while the Dharma was not the teachings I had once read about, but the truth that was hidden within all that is, and that expressed the Buddha. The Sangha, which was my precious support within the practice, was still an external support, but the division between it and me was getting more and more blurred -because it was getting clearer that it, like everyone and everything else, was a creation of my mind. So I felt a growing intimacy, a togetherness, beyond the conventional, as the Sangha and I not only became more and more at one, but expressed both the Dharma and the Buddha as well.

I therefore found that it was a question of nurturing my relationship with the three jewels through a willingness to surrender, rather than 'going for refuge' more and more, on a deeper level. Going for refuge was, for me, something to be cultivated, not something that paid much attention to formal recitation. It was much more about carrying around the warmth of feeling that my whole faith and trust could be handed into something that was not so much three refuges now, but one. And it was the trust that the refuges would support and carry me through any difficulties caused by fear of giving up the self and ego, that helped me to go, little by little, beyond the habits of attachments. It would be my faith in the three jewels that I trusted to 'catch' me as I practised turning away from the created world and my attachments over and over again. It was this developing intimacy with the three jewels that was crucial to my ability to let go. Letting go of all those things that make 'me' up: attachment to my views and opinions – driven by the passions and negative emotions – that were so vital to my sense of self and ego and that continually affirmed it.

Those who are new to the practice, but also perhaps many who have been practising for some time, may not be able to relate to this, or find anything of use for themselves, in reading about my relationship with the three jewels. But let it be an indication of the spirit of cultivating going for refuge. Maybe going for refuge now is much more objective and conceptual for you, but the spirit of going for refuge is to become more and more intimate with this 'concept' until it becomes your own living reality.

The Bodhisattva

For me, one of the great advantages of the bodhisattva path is that this type of practice can be applied in all the situations that life in our culture can present us with. The bodhisattva practice encourages us to take on board all of life's experiences, whatever they may be, and use them all as grist to the mill. Of course, quiet times and restraint need to be nurtured, for without them there is little meaningful meditation, but as most our life is spent *off* the cushion, this Path is much more appropriate to the non-monastic – and therefore the ideal practice for most of us.

However, a fundamental distortion can arise if there is a belief that bodhisattvas are interested solely in liberating beings from samsara whilst having little regard for their own personal insight, understanding, and release from suffering.

A fact of the bodhisattva path is that it is not actually possible to be of real spiritual use to other beings until you first know yourself deeply, and that requires you to give priority to your practice. Don't misunderstand me. I am not saying 'forget others, just focus on yourself'. The bodhisattva path is the practice of the great vehicle, and that means we take on not just ourselves, not just other beings, but also the totality of life. We cultivate an openness to engage with life as wholeheartedly as possible, because true understanding, and our true home, is in life in its totality.

Skilful practice involves getting our priorities right, and that means putting the practice of knowing ourselves foremost. This means living a life that allows us the time and space to return to our inner 'home' over and over again during our daily life. Do not feel that living your life exclusively for others is what the bodhisattva life is about. 'Charity begins at home': you have to be prepared to give yourself the space, in a consistent way, to stay with yourself, even when it may not be what you want to do or may even be frightening for you. Otherwise you will never see into yourself deeply enough to be of any real use to others – never mind being able ultimately to realize the final act of the bodhisattva and release all sentient beings from samsara. Reflect on the life of the Buddha, or indeed many, of the well-known figures in the history of Buddhism. They all spent many years working on themselves alone before returning to the community to help guide others in their practice. I'm not saying we should all take to the forests or mountains. But we do need to understand that there is much more to the bodhisattva path than a two-dimensional image of it may lead us to believe.

I wonder how many people, after reading descriptions of bodhisattvas, could imagine them as ordinary people, maybe someone you may meet on the bus, or stand next to in the supermarket checkout queue? Yet the being that has returned to his or her original nature after many years of practice, who then is reborn as a bodhisattva, is someone with more apparent contradictions than the average person could ever possibly create for themselves, however much they may try. Imagine someone who lives and functions in the world, who still retains likes and dislikes, but with the difference of knowing the 'reality' of these likes and dislikes and so less likely to grasp at them and turn the wheel of becoming. Imagine both a knowledge that is deep and unknowable to the 'worldly man' (and is unlikely to be seen unless asked for) and someone who is very ordinary and down-to-earth, someone who is working through and transforming habit and energy in just the same way as the 'ordinary' practitioner on the Path does.

In this aspect of training the bodhisattva is identical to the aspirant who cultivates the qualities and understanding that one day will allow him to alight upon the true bodhisattva path that leads to full and complete enlightenment. The bodhisattva is very much connected to life and this world is more normal and grounded than you may imagine. We should not therefore be put off by the images that have been created over time. Don't think you are not worthy or capable of such lofty idealism.

Another advantage of this path is its robustness. This gives us the perfect opportunity to work with the powerful negative self-view that obsess and weigh down most of us Westerners. The all-inclusive nature of this Path encourages us to bring our relationships with others, as well as with ourselves, into the practice; it encourages us to develop the spirit of making friends with all that we are. Often we buy into some familiar negative self-view that splits us down the middle and creates still more conflict. This adds to the heavy psychological weight that so many of us are familiar with. As understanding deepens, we learn to love ourselves more and more; accepting ourselves the way we are gives us a platform of equanimity from which we can move ever more deeply into the process of Dharmic change.

My own experience of treading the Path of the bodhisattva journey is that it is not really the mystery often portrayed in the scriptures, but a very down-to-earth way of practice – yet one that is forever revealing the secrets of life. Its spirit is not to push away what we consider to be unwholesome but rather to contain it whilst it is transformed. When the 'dark' has transformed, it will unite with the 'light' – which by then we shall understand more deeply – and go beyond even that unity where we will discover the full wonder of what we truly are.

The Framework of Practice

I would now like to touch briefly on the framework of practice that makes up the path of the aspiring bodhisattva. This framework, if it is correctly created and nurtured, will soon support and carry practitioners to the actual bodhisattva path, and, beyond the cycle of eternal becoming in which we are all caught up.

There are two fundamentals at the heart of Dharma practice: awareness of ourselves in all four postures of being (standing, walking, sitting, and lying down – as Buddhism defines our physical experiences of being) and the ability to use that awareness to look into ourselves and see the reality that lies beyond the world the deluded mind has created. In a way, that is all. There are no other factors involved. It is as simple as that. The fact that we cannot perform this simple act, and find that we have to employ all sorts of skilful means in order to accomplish it, does not diminish the ultimate simplicity of Dharma practice.

It is a fact that we cannot stay in a state of self-awareness, which is necessary for insight to arise, for more than a few seconds. That state of self-awareness means, for example, that when drinking a cup of tea you know you are drinking that tea, staying with that experience in its totality without mentally wandering off. This wandering off is, of course, what will happen, only for you to discover when you come back that you have drunk the tea and have little recollection of the experience. This same loss of awareness applies when you walk down the road and realize you are now at the end, and you have little recollection of taking the walk or any engagement with the environment that must have taken place. The same is true of all the endless flow of engagements with life: there is in truth very little consistent self-awareness.

Most of our life takes place on autopilot, while we are engaged with our chattering mind. It is because of this that we experience a lack of wholeness in our lives, and this is the reason for the existential dilemma of unfulfilment and incompleteness that we experience. The cultivation of being with our awareness, and thereby becoming whole and fulfilled, is what the eightfold path is for.

We need to tame the chattering mind for sure, but we need also to tame what drives it – our 'life-energy', that which keeps us alive and is what we really are. If left alone the chattering mind will rise and pass away second by second. But this doesn't happen because when thoughts arise there arises an identification with those thoughts, an identification that is created by the sense of self and ego that arises in the life-energy and so distorts it. If that sense of self and ego doesn't get its way, it will employ the life-energy itself in its efforts to make its will predominate. The life-energy, that in its essence is our original nature, now gets lost in this delusion of a self and ego which in turn becomes ever more harmful. The warm emotions of the heart become negative and transform into the destructive passions of greed, hatred, and delusion, the three passions that characterize the life of the self and ego. It is from this that the wheel of suffering is created, and it is this that we need to contain and transform by complete practice of the bodhisattva path.

We have to work on that destructive wilfulness of self and ego in order to attain a still mind that will give rise to the awareness we need in order to see into and beyond this sense of self and ego. We therefore cultivate the limb of ethics and conduct, a long training of restraining these negative outflows through containment. This containment is not oppressive, nor does it mean we have to turn away from our experiences of life in order not to be carried away, far from it. We learn to contain these destructive outflows by making use of the negative precepts of not taking life, not engaging in wrong speech, etc. We also bring into our life positive precepts such as helping others, engaging in skilful speech, etc., actions that nurture the natural warmth of the human heart. These precepts represent a turning away from the old habits of destructive self-interest and nurture new habits. These newly acquired Dharmic skills harmonize with our own heart's natural state, which compassionately uses them to help others.

As well as the support and guidance of the precepts, the skilful cultivation of an appropriate meditation practice can also be used. The four doctrinal concentration practices, also known as the sublime states, are traditionally used for this purpose. They are equanimity (upekkha), sympathetic joy (mudita), compassion (karuna), and loving kindness (metta) – and together they make up what are known as the Brahma Viharas. The loving kindness or metta meditation is the most commonly used. The great value of a meditation like metta is threefold. Firstly, it promotes the opening of the heart to other living beings. Secondly, it has the immense benefit of nurturing the meditator's positive feelings towards themselves, thus developing self-esteem (for we Westerners do have this propensity to dislike our self-image, and carry around such a negative, heavy burden of self, the like of which, I'd hazard, has never been known in the history of Buddhism). This nurturing of metta through meditation can also harmonize with the loving kindness nurtured towards ourselves whilst practising in daily life through our containment practice. Thus we naturally make friends with ourselves because of this developing non-judgemental relationship.

What we gain from this most important aspect of practice is making friends with ourselves, indeed learning to love ourselves, through a willingness to stay with and embrace an experience of ourselves that we have hitherto reacted against. By staying with those outflows of body, speech, and mind, we are 'repairing' our broken heart by bringing back into a whole the countless, fragmented pieces that create the conflict and negativity we feel. It will be true metta because it will be born of seeing and understanding ourselves – thus making it wisdom. When we love ourselves we will naturally love others, it will be impossible not to.

The third value of metta meditation is that, because the mind is more at peace with itself, it also helps train it in the stillness necessary for the Dharma to arise. So this is very much a training of a positive wholehearted engagement with life, so that we come to harmonize more and more as every day passes with our true nature, which is one of love for all that is.

This turning away from the blinding passions, and taming those negative outflows, slowly clear the mind of the inevitable turbulence and allow it to discover its natural quietness more and more. We help this cultivation along with meditation that promotes stillness and awareness. Stillness and awareness become more and more one, as the fruit of both is the same. With stillness, the awareness that is now stronger than ever can begin to look through all those thoughts and activities with skilful insight tools and see the truth of the world that grasps us all. Little by little, as it sees deeper and deeper, as it journeys through the world, little bits of 'me and mine' drop off because they no longer deceive. Finally the world stills and its power, which we so invest in, fades. It is then that awakening will take place – which is an absolute, concrete guarantee. When you 'recover' and return to life, you can embark on the inconceivable journey through the ten stages of bodhisattvahood, until the end of the Path is finally reached, and your initial awakening becomes final and complete – and so attain Buddhahood.

Eightfold Practice

Whatever Buddhist tradition you follow, and indeed whatever system of practice you follow within that tradition, you will find that all traditions, without exception, are grounded in the noble eightfold path, the fourth of the Buddha's four noble truths. It is this path of the practice of the Buddha-Dharma that is the heart of Buddhism. And it is this that those who wish to put an end to the cycle of suffering and rebirth need to practise, and need to practise in its totality, if the noble desire to put to an end this eternal cycle of becoming is to be fulfilled.

The path, for convenience and ease of understanding, is divided into the three limbs or sections of sila, translated as ethics or conduct, samadhi, which means a one-pointed mind born of concentration and mindfulness, and prajna, which mean wisdom or 'knowing how things really are'.

Sila is universal to all forms of Buddhism – indeed there is little difference between religious or spiritual movements as regards this aspect of the path. It consists of humanizing ourselves by containing and restraining self-interest and the destructive outflows – our habitual way of being. Indeed, the laws of the land demand that we maintain a certain degree of sila.

Samadhi is the cultivation of the ability to stay in a state of one-pointed self-awareness, to know ourselves from moment to moment in whatever situation we find ourselves. The foundation of this development is laid in our meditation, where we learn to disengage from our continual mental chatter and contain the negative emotional outflows and passions, thus enabling us to bring ourselves back, again and again, to the centre of our self-awareness. The ways to develop this ability may vary from tradition to tradition and from school to school, but they all lead to the same stillness.

Prajna is the ability to look into our being and see the reality of it, going beyond our deluded misinterpretation of that truth. The way to the discovery of the truth is to take a particular form of insight meditation – the one that is the way of the tradition and school we have chosen. All insight practices will at least seriously undermine the delusion that envelops us.

But what is this great delusion common to us all, that blinds us to the truth of the way things really are? It is the delusion of a self or ego, and the world of attachments that this sense of 'me and mine' creates. The practice of the eightfold path will take us to the root of this delusion, and destroy it.

The Buddha spent nearly fifty years travelling around India teaching the eightfold path as the way out of dukkha. He didn't say that to be ethical alone would be enough, and he didn't say that to perfect samadhi and enter even the highest dhyanas (concentrations) would be enough either. And he didn't say that just studying and understanding all that goes in the name of wisdom would be good enough. He taught that to be able to get to the root of dukkha, and to stop forever the experience of dukkha, it was absolutely necessary to embrace and practise the whole of the path. Ultimately, each of the eight steps of the path come into perfect balance and merge to become one.

1. Sila. right speech, right action, right livelihood
Many practitioners focus much of their time and energy observing the precepts of ethical behaviour, usually the negative precepts – inasmuch as they see to it that they don't fall into the crude actions that characterize many people. Those with more rounded practices observe these restraints but also cultivate aspects of what are termed the positive precepts. These include cultivating wholesome activities that engage them with the world, activities that stem from kindness and generosity, harmonious speech and a display of contentment with their life as reflected in a peaceful occupation.

For many, it has to be said quite frankly, this is really as much as they are capable of cultivating (or at least as much as they are prepared to commit themselves to). For some, it is not yet possible to sit quietly in meditation and cultivate the practices within that. If so, that is fine, and it is good that they surrender themselves as much as possible to the development of the ethical side of the practice. What is very helpful with this form of practice is also to cultivate the more ceremonial side of Dharma with puja and offerings to the Buddhas and Bodhisattvas – thereby cultivating both spirituality and faith as a further way of opening the heart. This helps nurture faith in the Buddha and his teachings, weakening a habitual idea that their practice is a thing to be grasped at.

For those who desire to put an end to dukkha, this is not enough. It is not enough to become a 'good' person. The Dharma will only really respond and show itself to those with a complete form of practice.

2. Samadhi. right effort, right concentration, right mindfulness

Deep concentration (samadhi) is possible when one has the ability to stay focused on a single object during meditation. There are many methods that can help us develop that ability. Each tradition usually has several ways, and each school within a tradition has its own focus on some of those ways. These can vary widely. There are the formless methods of anapanasati (the most widely-used method and common to all schools, and doctrinally the method used by all the Buddhas), translated as mindfulness of breathing, whereby we focus in different ways on our natural breathing without resorting to themes or concepts. Then there are the many conceptual methods of traditional Buddhism, and beyond them the visualization practices of Tibetan Buddhism and the koan and hua-do practice of Far Eastern schools that can act as both concentration and insight practices.

Whichever way we choose to go they all lead to the same goal; a mind that is awake through effort and concentrated. The practitioner is then centred and mindful within him or herself and totally alive to the present moment. This part of the path takes dedication and few people find it easy to still their chattering minds and contain the emotional outflows that continue to fuel those restless thoughts and mental pictures. There are also many who focus exclusively on this part of the path to the point that they turn away from the busy world and engagement with life as much as possible. They see that to really develop stillness it is skilful to turn away from distractions of the senses in order to go deeper. They understand that a practice of sila is very important too, in order to go deeper – for a mind that is agitated by unskilful acts gets in the way of the ability to attain stillness. So these people practise two thirds of the path, but this is not enough to impress the Dharma, because the Dharma will only really respond and show itself to those with a complete form of practice.

3. Prajna. right view, right resolve

The third part of the eightfold path is prajna or wisdom and 'knowing the way things really are'. It is often portrayed as the final part of the path to develop. When I look back over the years at the some of the teachers I've heard, and the practitioners I've encountered, it would not be difficult to draw the conclusion that Dharma practice is really more about sila and samadhi. I am still mystified as to why so many Dharma teachers seem to go down that route when it is clear they are leaving out the most important part of the eightfold path, because it is prajna, and only prajna, that takes the Dharma-farer beyond dukkha. It is only wisdom that breaks the taproot of ignorance. This was the main reason the Buddha took himself around India to teach for all those years. Sila was already established in his time, as was samadhi. It was samadhi in which Shakyamuni quickly became an expert in after taking instruction from the finest teachers of his day, yet he felt there was something missing from the 'wisdom' he attained from these practices. It was the feeling that there was something missing that drove him to seek further knowledge, eventually by himself, until one day, after nearly dying in the process, he attained the middle way and the ultimate understanding of life and death. It is the Buddhist expression of this understanding that sets Buddhism apart from all other religions, yet still some ignore this aspect of the Path.

Wisdom should be cultivated from the first day of practice, and it is the slow nurturing of wisdom that produces right view. Right view is ever-changing and deepening, but this deepening can only mature if we have the correct attitude. It isn't an intellectual wisdom but deeply personal and emotional – and requires that we be prepared to change and let go of the old 'me'. It is right resolve that allows this change to happen, and the deepening to take place.

Sila will make you an ethical being. Samadhi will give you peace and happiness, but it is wisdom that will make you a truly rounded human being because it is wisdom, and wisdom only, that will release the heart from the bondage of self-interest and non-understanding.

4. Complete

If we were to lay out the path in a linear fashion we could say the Path starts with sila, and then when that is refined the foundation for samadhi is laid, because to cultivate a still mind our general conduct has to be balanced – though not necessarily perfectly so. If we are engaged in crude activities the mind (which is of course integral to those activities) will not be capable of stillness, because we can't harness and tame the coarse emotional outflows associated with crude activities. When the stillness of mind has reached an acceptable degree, this becomes the foundation for prajna. Insight can shine through because the 'agitated waters of delusion' have stilled enough for the innate wisdom to rise up and shine through that stillness.

This is the linear form that many involved with teaching the Dharma seem to follow. But the fourth noble truth is subtler than the eightfold path formula might seem at first sight to suggest, and requires a subtler and more rounded presentation. This is because the fourth noble truth isn't, strictly speaking, the eightfold path at all, it is the middle way.

A new-born bodhisattva, whilst abiding in the bliss and wonder at the beginning of the bodhisattva path, sees, among the many insights that are revealed, the four noble truths as a direct seeing into the nature and framework of samsara. They are not seen as a formulation derived from the insight – some sort of summary of the nature of suffering. No, they are seen as a direct comprehension of the very nature of the construct of the deluded mind. And while comprehending samsara, and seeing that it is a complete fabrication of the deluded mind, the four truths are also 'seen'.

The truth is that every last part that goes to make up this invention of the world is completely and always saturated with dukkha. Not one speck is ever without dukkha. From this starting point it is understood that there is a cause or creator of this world. The second truth terms this desire, and it is the sense of a self or ego that creates that desire – thus creating the dualistic world-view with its perpetual drive for self-gratification and affirmation. Thus it is seen that the world and desire and dukkha are really just one.

When the creator of the world and of dukkha is known, the third truth is seen – that there is a way out of this mess, which is to destroy that creator. Finally, from this truth comes the way out of that bondage and entrapment. By resisting the pull of opposites that creates the dualistic world and which gives rise to the conditions for the phenomenon of a self or ego to arise, we can abide on the middle path between these opposites. By breaking our habitual running after things – which creates and engages us with the opposites of wanting and rejecting, liking and disliking, etc. – we starve that sense of self of its very lifeblood.

I would suggest that the eightfold path as we know it came about through the course of time, through the Buddha teaching and encouraging the practice of the middle way, through meditation and daily living. He would have broken down the middle way so that his listeners could relate to it and cultivate skilful ways of practice to achieve that noble end.

As is typical of our deluded mind, the parts which made up the whole soon came to be seen as sort of autonomous aspects of the practice of the fourth noble truth and became disconnected from that whole. Ultimately, parts of the whole were simply ignored, or at best given just the occasional glance. This lack of insight is not a true understanding of the fourth noble truth.

I'd like to stress again that though sila and samadhi can rightly be seen as the framework for wisdom, true practice is the cultivation of all the aspects of the path concurrently. In developing sila we resist our habitual desires and aversions and the trouble that this causes for ourselves and for others, and we cultivate and nurture the qualities of the unfettered human heart as the way forward. Resisting and containing our habitual actions is also the essence of the practice of sila that nurtures the stillness of mind that enables us to bring samadhi into our practice. The essence of samadhi is therefore identical to sila if it is seen as resisting the temptation to wander off and get caught in the created world of thoughts, mental pictures, and their associated passions. With these two limbs in place prajna itself has the space to arise, as it is only in a mind that is still that it has the conditions it needs. The arising of prajna then helps cultivate still more sila and samadhi. Cultivated sila and cultivated samadhi are not separate from prajna but are prajna itself, as any experienced meditator will confirm, so the turning to one's own prajna in meditation can often bring an instantly concentrated mind. So stillness and wisdom can be seen to be not just interconnected but identical in their essence. The apple tree and the apple itself are not separate.

The fourth noble truth is the middle way. It is not eight parts but one, which we pull apart and define in order to understand what it really is, and how we can proceed to attain that lofty state. If we get on with our practice with that in mind we will not get trapped into thinking that Dharma practice is only about being good, or that Dharma practice is only about bliss and happiness, or that Dharma practice is only about somehow understanding wisdom that we read and hear about. It is about the cultivation of the path in equal proportions. If your practice is truly balanced, then in quiet moments it should be possible, while pondering on any one of its aspects to see that aspect as containing all the others. Look at any one of the eight steps and you should be able to see the other seven in the very same place.

The ultimate seeing of the bodhisattva seeing the interpenetration of formations, that part of the doctrine that the ordinary mind cannot ever comprehend. The doctrine says that any one dharma contains all other dharmas throughout the entire universe and beyond, and yet that very same dharma retains its individuality and uniqueness. It may not be possible for you to see that truth fully, but if you can look at any part of the path whilst pondering your practice and you see it containing the other seven, and being identical with them, you are very close to seeing that truth of interpenetration. You will be seeing the middle way, and there is only one middle way – not eight. When you see and know your practice to be this way, you are on the threshold of fulfilling and perfecting the fourth noble truth, which is the perfection of Dharma practice in the world. Very soon after this, the samsaric world that you have been enslaved by since time began will abruptly cease, revealing reality in all its glory and majesty.

Practice in Everyday Life

Introduction

So far we have been looking at the basic tenets of the Path which most practitioners will be familiar with, but now I would like to offer you a bigger picture that takes the practice beyond the lists and formulas that can so easily keep us trapped inside our heads. We can kid ourselves with 'If I can just remember these often complicated formulas I will be understanding the Dharma and therefore making progress'.

One way I could describe the difference between the first part of the book and the second part is to say that part one was, in broad terms, about *WHAT* to do in terms of the practice, but here in part two it is more about *HOW* to practise.

After embarking on this 'living practice' it is often good to reflect on how we are experiencing our Dharma practice. We obviously learn as we move along, we start to see how we are so often at the mercy of our emotional states. Wisdom does indeed start to develop as we begin slowly to understand what makes us 'tick' and who we really are. The following reflections are to help us expand our awareness and understanding of the practice out of our heads and into the totality of our being. We can then live it out in the totality of life itself. The reflections can help us understand who we are and come alive to the whole spectrum of understanding that unfolds within this remarkably subtle practice.

Some of those who read the subtitle of this book will be disappointed if they are hoping to read something about sitting meditation. This subject is well covered in many books and I'm sure most who read this book will already have a good idea how to sit and how meditation works – you don't need any more from me. Of course sitting meditation is crucial to practice and it is the cornerstone of change, but here I'm encouraging the practitioner, in effect, to meditate throughout the day. In other words to be at one, mindful and centred, with what you are doing, no matter what that may be. I'm pointing towards what needs to be nurtured and guarded so that the worldly mind doesn't come and grab you off balance. I hope you will find useful pointers here on how to practise and break free.

Dharma Mind

A baby quickly realizes that crying when it is hungry or wants attention will soon lead to those desires being fulfilled. Self-interest begins to arise in these very early days of life, when an awareness of separateness begins to take shape, and from then on almost everything that being does will be driven by this sense of self-interest. Almost all the desires, aversions, and ambitions of that young life will be driven by an urge to become something – something that has a sense of a self at its root.

As adults we would do well to look into our own motivations. If we did we could quickly conclude that there is hardly anything that motivates us outside of this same self-interest, however subtle it may sometimes seem. Self-interest takes control of our lives to such an extent that we rarely experience anything beyond it.

For example, one day we discover Buddhism and the Dharma and we decide to take up a practice of the teachings – for whatever reason. Is this just another interest, like so many before? One in which we engage our self-interest in order to fill our time, or achieve something, or get a reward of some sort? If we approach our new interest in Dharma practice in the usual way with this 'worldly mind', I'm afraid we will stand little chance of gaining the spiritual maturity we may have wished for.

Our habits are deeply ingrained, so we may well start off with the wrong intentions for our practice of the Dharma. For example, we may want to become someone who will be admired and respected, for example, or become so wise that we can 'save' people and be admired still further. But coming to Dharma practice we need a totally different approach, and mind-set, to anything we have experienced or engaged in before in our entire lives. This is because the root of Dharma practice is ultimately not about becoming anything at all, but about unbecoming. This mind is called Dharma mind.

The heart and spirit of Dharma practice is about learning to surrender, and giving up our ingrained habitual self-interests. So rather than seek any reward in our new practice, we begin to cultivate a spirit of not wanting anything in particular in return for our efforts. Just cultivating this attitude and giving up those precious attachments will now be reward enough. With this practice, the one desire that is allowed by the Dharma – the noble desire for release from suffering – can be fulfilled. This new mind and its cultivation require a seismic change of attitude.

In fact, this change of attitude has to be learned and relearned, over and over again, as we continually fall back into our old habits of seeking reward. Thoughts such as 'if I'm going to do this practice, I want to become like this and not any longer be like that' creep in. This ingrained habit of self-interest is so powerful that we fall back into its clutches over and over again. But learning to give up, to surrender all those self-interests, within the practice of a wholehearted commitment to life, will in itself remind us that this is the way of the Dharma.

The way of the Dharma is not the way of the world. The way of the world is to want and become, the way of the Dharma is to give up and unbecome. This cultivation takes faith in the teachings, and faith in the three jewels. The fear of 'If I am no longer going to be like this and I am no longer wanting to become like that, what will become of me?' is the fear that brings us back, again and again, to the self-interest of wanting to be something. But it is faith in the three jewels of the Buddha, Dharma, and Sangha, faith that we have nurtured since the beginning of our practice, that will support and carry us through that fear. So we will discover that, far from the black hole, and even death, that we fear will overtake us if we give up all desires, the human heart will shine through and take the place of fear and self-interest. It will shine through and radiate all around with warmth and love because it is now a heart that is free from the bonds of desire and self-interest.

Staying at Home

It has been interesting, but sometimes alarming, at the book launches and in private talks, to hear others talk about their meditation experiences. I get particularly alarmed, when I am told of experiences of energy gathering during sits – energy that runs through the body – perhaps finding its way to the head, or into a limb, or even to an internal organ, sometimes causing violent jerking of the body or limbs, or just general pain and discomfort. Sometimes that energy, having nowhere to go, even seems to create mental images of devils and demons.

From the reports it seems to be of no particular importance what the meditation subject is – there have been many techniques developed over the centuries in Buddhism, but despite their variety they still fall into two basic categories, concentration and insight – as it appears problems can arise whatever type of meditation is being practised. Concentration, however, is a necessary feature of both.

The basis of most of the problems I hear brought up are, I am sure, based on the assumption that the Dharma is to be found in our heads and intellect – through energetic thinking and working things out. And so we ignore the body. This is the conclusion to which my observations of Buddhists over the years has led me. Whilst the intellect does have a big part to play in clarifying our understanding of the journey that we are embarking upon, its true part in the scheme of things is essentially not to discover wisdom but to orientate us to where wisdom awaits our discovery. That is in the body.

Those who have a desire for complete understanding need to discover where the home of the Dharma lies. With this knowledge, we will fully incorporate the body into our practice, to harmonize it with the intellect and so nurture the integration of mind and body. We involve our body through learning to understand and engage with the emotional energy that drives our desires. Our emotions gather and are experienced in the part of the body below the navel; in Far Eastern Buddhism this is often called the hara or 'seat of the emotions'. This part of our body is the most crucial part to understand if we are really to integrate mind and body and create a complete and well-rounded practice.

In order to understand the crucial part the hara plays in our practice we need to focus on it as much as possible. This was something I fortunately learned to do from the beginning of my Dharma training. Our attention is naturally drawn there during a strong emotional experience when we might feel discomfort, or even pain, there. I could see that this area contained great energy that would fuel my desires and aversions and give those experiences the drive and momentum needed to keep them strong. I learned to give this area much attention as I could clearly see that it played a major part in what I really am. A major discovery was that this was potentially an area of tremendous power, and that if I didn't learn to harness that power it could easily run into the body and cause physical problems. This emotional energy was a part of the overall energy that gave me life, and it needed to be healthy and in a balanced state or it could quite easily bring physical (and mental) damage.

I discovered that if I learned to keep my awareness there as much as possible, my understanding of myself deepened very quickly. It became clear to me through that deepening understanding that this was in fact where I really was, and not in the head, 'up there', as I had always assumed. This realization clearly showed me that this is where the Dharma arises too, where it is to be found. With this knowledge I could see the preciousness of staying with my awareness as much as possible right there in my body, and I came to see the hara as my home.

My practice from then on was always to be 'staying at home', as much as my chattering and deluded mind would allow, to catch myself wandering over and over again, and then return home and stay at home for as long as I could. What a place to be! Here is where the driving emotional life-energy gathers. (I much prefer to call the emotional energy 'life-energy' – or even 'life-force' – rather than just 'energy'. To say just 'energy' could suggest that it is just a dead force, something that could even be seen as coming from outside and not really part of me at all, whereas in reality we are so intimately connected with it that a division can't be found.) By staying at home I soon discovered that this is actually where I am and that same place is also where the Dharma is to be discovered. So neither the Dharma nor I are up there in my head, as my intellect is continually trying to convince me that they are.

My discoveries continued as it became obvious that the world I was creating was driven by this life-energy, as was my sense of self and the suffering which all of that brings. The life-energy wasn't the world or the self as such, but its power gave those creations the life they needed. It became clear that the way forward was not to assume that the insight process was purely mental, but to see it as physical also. It was essential to contain that life-energy, so as to allow the maturing insight faculty to transform the delusion of self and other in a full and proper way.

So here in the hara we have the main focus for the complete practice of the bodhisattva path. We should make it our 'home', as we need to focus and abide here so that we can learn, through right practice, to contain that emotional flow. This allows the precious transforming process to take place, through the power of wisdom, thus freeing us of the ignorance that permeates our whole being.

Because we are physically still, and more especially mentally still, during meditation, the build-up of the life-energy – especially when deeply concentrated – can be more acute than usual. Because it cannot flow in any of its usual ways through our normal physical or mental activities, it creates these experiences I mentioned at the start of this section. It becomes essential, through experience, to learn to contain this life-energy. We need to allow the charged life-force to do its job and move safely through our being as we live our life, rather like restraining an untamed horse with a rope as you train it to become gentle. Allow it to move and express itself as a strong and healthy animal, but in a contained and controlled way. With this in place we can avoid the traumas touched on earlier.

The way to work with this danger that all meditators face is to be aware of it and train yourself to keep your awareness centred within the hara. Always give it your utmost attention, return and abide there over and over again, right in the depths of your body. Train yourself to stay at home. Become aware of the wandering life-energy with your mind, and then harness it with that same awareness and drag it back to the centre and your home – so preventing it running through the body causing problems. By cultivating this awareness, the energy eventually shouldn't impinge on your meditation at all and it should be possible to stay centred and develop the meditation at the same time.

So whatever meditation you may be doing, make the hara your home. Take yourself there whenever you can. Take your meditation there and bring the two together – even if you consider yourself to be contemplating something more mental – don't consider yourself abiding separately from your body and be up there in your mind. By staying at home you are abiding in the practice centre of your being. By centring yourself there you are gathered up in a controlled and balanced state, so that when the life-energy wants to wander off in its frustration at its containment you can catch it quickly and drag it home again.

I have highlighted this experience by focusing on it whilst in meditation but it should be noted that it is equally essential to cultivate that awareness and containment in your daily life as well, as I have explained in the 'Containment in Everyday Life' section.

Those on the bodhisattva path should soon come to realize that this path is actually much more of a physical practice than a mental one – because we are actually transforming the errant life-energy which is where the presence of ignorance manifests, creating the samsaric world we are all bound to. All this transformation takes place in the body, because it is the Dharma that does the transforming and it is in the body, and in the essence of life, where the Dharma is to be discovered. With our awareness, whose essence and centre is in the body, it should be possible to remain in contact with the body at all times, and stay more and more in the body as our practice develops. We can then stay with those powerful forces that we need to contain to enable the transforming process to take place. As we learn to stay at home, we are not only safe from the danger of being taken into the clouds by our deluded mind, but also stand a much better chance of not succumbing to many physical and mental sicknesses.

Practice in Lay Life

I was often asked during question-and-answer sessions if it is really possible to practise in lay life, especially in a large, busy city such as London. We often view the practice of a traditional monk, who spends his time away from the hurly-burly of lay life, as in many ways more ideal. During my short time in robes in Sri Lanka I never had to worry where the next meal would come from, or if there would be a problem in replacing my worn out robes, or where the money would be found to repair the leaking roof of my hut. All my basic requisites were provided when necessary by the lay sangha that so generously supported the ordained sangha. Because I was totally free from having to consider the basics of life I was able to focus on my practice without distraction. For example, I could meditate for many hours a day, which would not be possible to do in lay life simply because I would have to go out and earn my living. So we might consider that lay existence not only severely impairs our practice, but in the view of many that I have met, especially in the Theravada sangha in Sri Lanka, renders deep penetration into the Dharma impossible. All I can say about it is that from my own direct experience of years of practice that notion is not at all correct.

There could be a question mark over the feasibility of practice in lay life if one is pursuing types of practice that need extreme stillness and quiet, and where normal engagement with life is seen as a hindrance. But the bodhi-sattva path – which is the one that I practise and is the only Path that I concern myself with and encourage others to pursue, is most definitely possible in lay life, for the bodhisattva path is the path of totality and has no time for dualistic discriminatory attachments, but takes on all of life, whether it is robust or quiet, and uses it all as grist to the mill. The bodhisattva path is the path that leads to Buddha nature, and one of the marks of Buddha nature is that it *is* the totality of life. If you wish to see Buddha nature then any thoughts of dissecting life into convenient parts has to be abandoned. Cultivating the spirit that wisdom is to be found in all situations is the way forward with this practice of totality.

While daily practice is crucial, in a non-monastic life there should always be time to gather up all those experiences to reflect upon and digest all those weeks and months of practice. You can use that new-found ability to deepen practice by taking regular retreats. After all, monks take them as well! If you see the retreat as a continuum of your daily practice there should be a feeling of seamlessness as you embark upon this special time. Retreats are indeed very special on your spiritual journey, but they have an inherent danger in much the same way as focusing too much on sitting meditation during your everyday life. The completeness of Dharma understanding can only be attained through consistent practice throughout the whole day, but a trap that many fall into is the thought that 'if I just pile up my meditation mileage that will be all I need for enlightenment.' The same trap also applies to retreats. How often people think 'Well, if

I meditate a bit that should be good enough because I'm off on retreat soon so that should take care of any inertia and any lack of commitment that I now have towards the practice.' This is very much a wrong understanding. Whatever meaningful breakthrough may be experienced on retreat is very much the fruit of daily commitment that matures during those precious days of extraordinary commitment – commitment that is not possible on a normal daily basis. So make use of retreats as yet another aspect of practice that compensates for the lack of advantages of a secluded life.

To contain and delve into the power and robustness that characterizes much of lay life represents a precious opportunity to practise. With this in mind, it could even be said that lay life is better for practice than monastic life. It is clearly a much more robust practice but a practice that is therefore also fraught with many more dangers. It is robust because we obviously have to deal with the powerful situations with which life can present us with, for example in human relationships, or just the general grind of trying to lead a normal existence. It is fraught with dangers because we are continually being tested and tempted to give way to the strong pull of desires thrust upon us by the very nature of our living in our society. This is why it is essential to know how to practise throughout the whole day while we are engaged with life. Use all these situations to develop containment and insight. It becomes essential in this kind of practice that we learn to cultivate skilful means in our lives – and to me the primary skill to learn is to learn to take control of your life.

It is a common experience of many people that with a hectic and pressured job, plus perhaps a family to look after, and other commitments, we seldom seem to get a minute to ourselves. We are pulled this way and that – hardly seemingly able, even, to take a breath. For the most part we are unable to change these circumstances, though we would often love to do so, simply because of the pressures in our life.

In order to practise correctly it is very important to become master of our circumstances rather than be pulled around by them. We need a measured day – where we can move from one task to another as easily as possible. Beyond that we need to create some space where we can relax and gather ourselves up, reflect and be with ourselves. If we are always running this way and that, it is never going to be possible to cultivate the essence of practice – which is to know ourselves whilst engaging with life. If our life is such that we cannot have the space and time on a daily basis that allows us to practise consistently and evenly, our practice will have no chance of maturing.

If our work doesn't allow that space we should make the utmost effort to create some at home. Try to rearrange the schedule and create time just to be with yourself and reflect not just on the day but get familiar with your reactions and feelings to it, and in many respects become reacquainted with yourself. I know there is meditation time for these things, but that can become just a part of the busy schedule as well, and just another thing that has to be done. Find the time to just quietly potter around, maybe do the dusting or some other job, read a book, or listen to the radio or, dare I say it, watch television. Be so that whatever you are doing you can be aware of yourself and get acquainted with the feelings and emotions that may arise during these times. Mull over the Dharma in your mind and see your connection with it, learn to enjoy your own company and be still. It is this developing skill in taking control and making space that compensates for the quietness that monks enjoy.

It can be that we become so used to interacting with others, busy and speeding around, that the prospect of just being with ourselves alone in our home can be a frightening prospect. Yes, you may say, 'but I am happy to sit by myself meditating quietly for an hour every day and I do have regular meditation retreats, therefore that is not a problem for me.' But how many of us, when we discover there is a gap in our diary, freeze at the thought that there will be nothing to do, and I'll be left all by myself, alone? Just the thought of being alone for even a short time can bring up such feelings of loneliness and fear that it can be very difficult to bear. By not giving in to the temptation to fill that time but learning to stay with that fear, to stay at home and open up to that experience whilst pottering around doing nothing in particular can become a great source of insight.

So you can see that taking control of your life, and building the determination to create skilful situations for practising the Dharma, not only allows us to create these precious periods of stillness and space in our hectic days, but also the possibility for insight to arise.

I would say, yes, most definitely it is possible to practise in lay life, to practise in the hectic pressured world of noise and pollution and the crazy people of big cities, to be able to stand in the middle of Piccadilly Circus and practise. It just requires commitment and the development of skilful means to make it possible.

Containment in Everyday Life
One of the most pleasing aspects of my book launches
and the question-and-answer sessions that would follow,
and indeed of the Dharma groups I been leading since
that time, is the number of times I have been asked to say
something about containment in daily life. To me this is
the area of practice that is so crucial to total transformation and yet little seems to be known about it. But as far
as total transformation is concerned – which is the main
characteristic of the bodhisattva path it needs to be
grasped and understood more clearly than any other
aspect of the practice.

Many of us who come to Buddhism have an image of
it as a practice of sitting meditation and very little else.
This wrong understanding is encouraged as so many of
the images associated with Buddhism are of the Buddha
sitting peacefully cross-legged. Most of us then, when we
come to Buddhism almost gravitate to meditation as soon
as possible and learn some sort of technique that we work
on and develop. There is so often this inevitable emphasis
on sitting meditation that somehow, if not quite seen as
the complete picture of practice, is seen almost as the
complete practice. Some forms of Buddhist practice
seem to lay almost exclusive emphasis on meditation,
with an element of sila in the background to help create
the equanimity conducive to good meditation. It then
really becomes a practice of meditation and cultivation of
an environment that will help with that practice, but the
bodhisattva path is not like that at all.

The bodhisattva path is about the total transformation of all that we are, which means that in order to walk and nurture that Path the practice needs to be cultivated in what is traditionally known in Buddhism as the four postures which characterize the experience of life. These are standing, sitting, walking, and lying down, all the four postures of being without seeing one posture as superior to another. The essence of this practice is to train ourselves to walk between the extremes of craving and rejection that characterize much of our lives, to remain in the place we call the middle way. In order for that to happen our training will have to take place and be consistent throughout the whole day in all situations, whether good or bad, pleasant or unpleasant etc. It is of no consequence what the situation is, as the Dharma is present in every moment, and is always waiting to be discovered. It is our job to discover it.

It has been interesting to observe over these past years, in the West and indeed in the East, how easy it has become to walk in off the street, so to speak, into a meditation centre and be taught a technique in a few days. We can then just walk out again – with little reference made to the necessity of to create a daily practice away from the sitting, so as to support and complement the difficulties inevitably experienced in deepening what has been learned. Apart from an essential daily practice there is also, for example, the need for a sangha to support this new practice. This is not an optional add-on, if it happens to be convenient or if you feel like it. Going for refuge to the sangha is a part of the going for refuge to the three jewels, and the side-stepping of one of the three jewels takes the practice outside the parameters of the eightfold path, so genuine and permanent change is not going to be possible. I would even go as far as to say that a being of deep spiritual understanding doesn't ever really go beyond the need for sangha either. To be apart from like-minded people could affect his well-being as he wouldn't be able to share his understanding through associating with like-minded people.

Soon after coming to the Dharma we are generally taught that the way forward is through our meditation. We know that we are trying to remain in a state of one-pointed awareness – by coming back to our meditation subject the moment we catch ourselves wandering off into thoughts and mental pictures. We soon discover this is not an easy exercise to perform. After a short while we go a bit beyond our practice of coming back to our centre after thoughts and mental pictures have carried us away; we start having to deal with negative feelings that now begin to impinge. Gone is the 'honeymoon' of the novelty, now negative feelings of restlessness begin to arise. These feelings create thoughts and mental pictures to accompany them, so that not only do we get lost in thoughts and mental pictures again but this time there is some sort of negative emotional power behind them as well. We now find it more difficult to catch ourselves and bring ourselves back to the centre of awareness, as these negative emotions makes our loss of awareness more acute. So what may have started out as an easy, pleasant exercise in peace and quiet now becomes something that requires more effort, but we muster up the determination to stay with our meditation subject and soldier on.

Just when we think we have got to grips with this new if slightly unpleasant dimension, a third factor arises that then takes us to the crossroads where we are presented with the reality of our commitment to meditation: the passions.

When these begin to arise they not only condition our thoughts and mental pictures to a great degree but engage the body much more than before because the passions are in essence more of a physical experience. Now we have much more to deal with than before, and our time spent trying to concentrate can be almost unbearable. The nature of our everyday mind abides in restlessness, just watch it and see how long it can stay with one thing. What that subject is is not very important; somehow it just has to wander off into something else even if only for a few seconds. Normally we live with this and accept that the mind spends just about every second of every minute chattering away to itself about everything and nothing. Through all this we carry on and live our lives for much of the time seemingly on automatic pilot because of this non-stop thinking, and consequently not really being aware of what we are doing in any given moment. When we decide to still that mind in meditation we soon discover the force that can arise if we don't give in and play its games of perpetual restlessness. If we do

manage to still thoughts and discover that precious stillness, negative emotional forces begin to gather and arise
from the pit of our stomach, or hara, and begin to inflame
our thoughts. We soon discover that this restlessness
becomes much more of a physical experience as these
emotional forces run through our body and manifest in
unpleasant ways. We twitch, we move, we scratch, we
look around, we blow our nose, we change our posture
and check the time, we find anything to relieve that
build-up of frustrated energy. Through perseverance and
a determination not to give in to these distractions, we
learn to bear with it and carry on bringing ourselves back
to the centre and remain one-pointed. Through time,
even if it's just a little, that negative emotional force loses
its power and calms down, it displays its inevitable impermanence. Feelings of happiness and even bliss can
then arise as we continue to stay one-pointed, allowing
us to bathe in the fruits of our efforts to stay with it. We
learn to stay with and bear with the arising of the passions. We learn to stay with what we are doing in the
moment, and that is staying centred in the coolness of
awareness even in the middle of all this mental and
physical dukkha – but can we do this in our everyday life?
Can we stay with what we are doing when we are engaged
in some mundane daily activity, when someone comes to
us whilst we are engaged in a particular activity and says
something unpleasant that pulls immediately at our feelings and emotions? Do we not straight away get caught
up and strike out verbally or otherwise? Or maybe we

buckle under to what is said and withdraw because we have heard an unpleasant truth about ourselves? Or if it's so unpleasant we may even turn away and suppress our feelings because we can't face the truth. There is always a reaction, and it is invariably driven by negative emotions or, worse, the passions, so when that experience arises we lose the ability to stay with what we are doing, and get lost in the clouds created by those reactions.

But remember, staying mindful and at one with this particular activity is no different from staying with the meditation subject while meditating. In our meditation we are always bringing ourselves back to the centre. Do you think that we should be doing something different when we are engaged in a daily activity?

In our meditation we learn to open up and bear with the emotions and passions that come up, and allow ourselves to burn up inside them without playing and being carried away with the games they create through thoughts and mental pictures. To practise the bodhisattva path fully and completely it is essential to see that the practice is exactly the same in whatever posture and activity we may be in, because the bodhisattva practice is the practice of totality.

This really is such a crucial feature of the complete training of the bodhisattva path that we need to explore and understand that we are actually transforming habits of a lifetime. We are stopping the wheel of causation from turning and returning it to its source, paradoxically, putting to an end the endless cycle of rebirth and an eternity of dukkha. Because it is such a lofty ideal, you may feel it needs a lot of Dharmic understanding and to be practised in special circumstances, but it doesn't. In fact it is in the ordinary where the practice is to be found, so ordinary and everyday that you may let the precious opportunity pass you by, because you feel that the ordinary is unimportant and not where the Dharma is. This is so wrong. Let's look at an everyday example: getting up in the morning to go to work.

Getting up to go to work is not something most of us find easy, and we certainly do not look forward to it most of the time. When we are woken up our practice starts just there, when the mind engages and thinks negatively about having to get out of that warm comfortable bed, but we still do. In doing this there may well be lots of not just mental resistance but also physical feeling and even unpleasant emotional feelings against having to do that. Maybe in the past we would have succumbed to those experiences and stayed in the warm and enjoyed our inertia, but now we are practising the Dharma so we don't give into them but do what we know we should be doing – getting up, and containing those forces.

We get up and get dressed and all the other things we do at this time and all the time contain those negative mental and physical experiences within the activities we are carrying out. We just carry out those activities as simply and as straightforwardly as we can, to the extent that anyone around us wouldn't even be aware of our internal resistance and turmoil.

In our meditation we come back to what we are meant to be doing at the time, which is remaining centred in awareness by catching ourselves when we become lost in thoughts and mental pictures, and also, crucially, containing the negative emotions and passions. Now that we are engaged in a daily activity, we are doing precisely the same thing. We come back through our awareness to stay mindfully with what we are meant to be doing – centred in the awareness of our activity.

Because our minds are continually engaged in thoughts and mental pictures it is unrealistic to try to extinguish them, but the passionate outflows are quite a different issue. These we can work on, and it is the taming of the passions and negative emotions and the transforming of them that will eventually take us out of samsara. It is the taming of the passions and negative emotions that is at the very heart of the bodhisattva training.

In the example we have been using, instead of giving in to the negative emotional desire to stay in bed, we don't allow it to take over but contain it and carry through with the activity we know should be done. This emotion can build to a passionate intensity to the extent that it becomes almost unbearable physical pain, usually centred on the hara – the seat of the emotions – in the lower abdomen. But rather than give in to it we learn to open up and surrender ourselves right into the heart of that physical experience with a willingness to burn up inside that fire. There will be thoughts and mental pictures continually trying to deflect us from our commitment, but we don't yield. But what are we really doing?

In a situation such as this we have finally decided not to buy into an old familiar situation and get carried away by that ingrained habit. We are not going to get carried away any more by the fire of those thought-habits and attachments, to likes and dislikes and our opinions about what is right and wrong and what we want and don't want. All those old familiar things only give us trouble and cause problems in life with others and ourselves. For once we are not going to give into that, that which turns the wheel of becoming and all the karma that accompanies it, that compels us to be the helpless participants in a world that is not conducive to happiness. We are surrendering ourselves. We are quite literally giving up this sense of self and 'me'. Giving all of ourselves up with a bright clear mind that is aware of all that is happening, that resists those habitual reactions and says 'yes' to all that arises from within the mind and which embraces and accepts without judgements and labels. There is a willingness to accept what we may not want to see, and a willingness to accept that this is a part of us, for good or bad, and to bear with all the force that drives it. We stay with our world and bear with it until eventually, because these forces are not being allowed to turn and perpetuate the karmic cycle any more, they gradually change and transform back into their true original nature, the true nature that expresses itself as a gentle and genuine human being, who is warm and at one with others and the wonder of life.

This example of getting up in the morning is simple, but it applies to all our everyday experiences; the same openness to, and containment of, the negative outflows is applied to everything, including the more complex experiences of human relationships. To open and accept, contain, and function in as human a way as we can, is the practice. This willingness not to play the game of spinning the wheel of becoming transforms the driving emotional passionate power that once was owned by the desires, back into its original nature, which then reacts spontaneously to the needs of mankind without any doer or desire for reward.

Kindness to All Things

Some may find it strange that not only is it part of our training to cultivate and nurture kindness and consideration and all that implies to sentient beings, but it is also a skilful practice to cultivate kindness to non-sentient things as well. Of course this wouldn't be fashioned with the same sensitivity we would have to other living beings, with all the considerations that would naturally include. But kindness, and even respect, for everything we encounter nurtures a kind heart in the same way as kindness to beings. When I first came to this practice I was working in Regent's Park in London as a gardener. We were expected to clean and oil the tools at the end of each day's work, even though the next day we would bring them out first thing and make them dirty again. The idea was that the tools would last longer and, there was also consideration and respect for the person who might wish to use the tools the following day, but for me it went deeper than just those issues. It became apparent to me that to nurture a respect for the tool itself was cultivating still further a spirit of sensitivity, in the knowledge that, whether animate or inanimate, we are all part of the whole, because Dharma practice is about nurturing the return to the wholeness of life where our original nature is to be found, as it is this that we lost when we took on a sense of self and created the experience of objects and separateness.

The return to our true nature is made possible by becoming proficient in meditation and through the development of insight into reality. As part of our developing understanding we see and acknowledge that to arrive at that end we need to develop skilful means in our dealings with others and the world, through wholehearted engagement, through openness and friendliness, because we see this as the expression of the heart's true nature. We readily nurture our innate human virtues, qualities, and potentials, so as to fulfil our practice. What we are doing with this engagement is learning to go beyond, not just our own sense of separateness but that of 'other' – through wholehearted commitment to practice. This will then bring us closer to our true nature. We need to go beyond even that separateness of self because we are part of a much bigger picture. In order to become truly whole again we need to nurture the spirit that we cultivate not just towards others and ourselves but also to the whole of life, including the non – sentient, because it is this totality that makes up the whole, and our true nature.

It is not enough just to engage with metta and develop loving kindness towards others. If you are really interested in the full reward of the bodhisattva path, expand that practice of consideration and respect to embrace the whole world and everything that is in it. Clean the tools you have used and return them to their rightful place. Drive your car with sensitivity and kindness. Do not throw and kick things because you are frustrated with them or make them the object of your frustration. Learn to be open to them and see them as your friends, see them as a vehicle to reality, part of the same mystery that you are.

It is said that people talk to plants. We don't have to take this literally of course but what is meant by this is that by stilling and opening up our minds to this form of life, our natural intuitive sensitivity is able to commune with plant and see their needs. This way of communicating is the real 'talking', and further cultivates the respect for all that is, a respect that leads to the experience of the oneness of life.

With this cultivation we are not just embracing humans and nurturing compassion for their plight, but embracing all that is, because we see that everything is a part of the whole. In the whole there isn't that which is alive and that which isn't alive. Wholeness is the Buddha nature itself, and it is within this true nature that all things have their home.

PRACTICE IN EVERYDAY LIFE

Mindfulness

I've read many books in which the terms awareness and mindfulness appear the same and are interchanged quite freely, but, I see a difference between them. They may well be the closest of friends and firmly linked, but they are different, and that difference is worth exploring. To state the difference at the outset I would say that awareness is fully alive but non-engaging and therefore passive (at least until the later stages of the bodhisattva path when separateness and duality cease), whilst mindfulness is fully alive and energetic.

Mindfulness is the conscious act of bringing ourselves back to the state of awareness. We use mindfulness as a tool; it is a conscious tool that we learn to employ with skilful means in meditation, and in everyday activities, to bring ourselves back to what we are engaged in. Mindfulness takes us back to where we are training ourselves always to be abiding – in a state of pure awareness. As most of us would readily admit, we are seldom fully conscious of what we are doing at any moment. How many times have we walked down a long road and reached the other end to realize we have no recollection whatsoever of the journey – and the engagement we must have had with the environment along the way?

And for those who drive a car, how many journeys across a busy town, stopping and starting, continually making decisions, have we taken and at journey's end had little recollection of it? often accompanied by the startling thought 'Did I drive through any red traffic lights?!'

We are all familiar with these experiences, yet it is the purpose of Dharma training for us to be alive and aware in the activity – however mundane – that we are doing right now. How can we achieve this?

In our meditation we have a technique that we concentrate on that allows us to develop the ability to stay one-pointed and in a state of awareness. To always be coming back to it when we wander off in thoughts and mental pictures – even if they are driven by the emotions and passions. We surrender to the activity of, say, counting the breath. It is the surrender to that activity that allows us to be alive to the moment. In our daily lives it is the same principle. If I am brushing my teeth I stay totally with that activity. I am aware of the feeling of the bristles passing over the teeth and gums, I am aware of the taste of the paste etc. I give myself to that experience but I have to bring forth mental effort to stay there, and sure enough however much I try to stay with it the mind kicks in and I'm off again into a thought and soon lose the awareness of the activity. But it is the ability to return, through mindfulness, that allows me to catch myself and bring myself instantly back into the aliveness of that moment. This coming back and wandering off and coming back again can happen several times just within this simple everyday activity, but it is the willingness, through mental effort and commitment, to engage in being at one with this that to me is the essence of mindfulness. It is a profoundly deep energetic mental commitment to the Dharma. It is the commitment to try to be alive to every activity. When sweeping the floor be mindful and with that commitment bring yourself back from your thoughts and become alive and aware to what you are doing.

How easy it is to go through the day and not remember that we are supposed to be practising the Dharma and so be aware and alive to the moment, all day thinking this and thinking that and never really experiencing the wonder of just being. A willing commitment to be mindful promotes the ability to train ourselves to come back home, to be always coming back to ourselves.

I have found, through experience, a way that helps to promote this ability. I realized that if this mind of mine must always be chattering, it would be best for it to chatter about something which would help lead me back to myself and awareness i.e. the Dharma. I then try if possible to go beyond that chattering mode and muse or ponder on the Dharma instead.

To muse, or ponder, is to go beyond our everyday normal thinking and 'look' and be aware of our subject with a bright, still mind. With this in place, you will find the pondering will begin to take place much more in the body than in the mind. This can become evident in meditation, but try it even whilst just coming and going in daily life. By musing beyond thought you are much more likely to be aware of yourself and the body. And with the essence of awareness being very much in the body, this musing or pondering is much more likely to go beyond the reach of the self and the distortions it may bring with it. This brings us closer to the Dharma, because truth is actually found deep within our own being.

If your Dharma knowledge is correct, your Dharmic thoughts should always promote a tendency to reflect on yourself. Whatever Dharmic subject you may wander off in, it should always be somehow linked to you, and be seen as something personal to relate to. There are aspects of Buddhist wisdom and ideas on which we can ponder that may take us outside of ourselves, often into the clouds. But for those who are committed practitioners the knowledge that we choose to think about or ponder upon should always have the effect of turning our attention inwards, should always be personal and lead to a connection within. If you are prepared to ponder only those matters that make you turn inwards, then you are just a moment away from catching yourself and returning to your self-awareness and to what you are doing just then. So ponder Dharma that turns you inward; do not ponder what you think to be Dharma that only serves to take you away.

If you are looking for something to ponder then may I suggest something that has been so useful for me, the most wonderful of contemplations, one that can be pursued both in the deepest samadhi and in the middle of the busiest high street, that is, to ponder the tilakkhana or three signs of being: anicca, dukkha, anatta – impermanence, unsatisfactoriness, and not-self or insubstantiality. At any time of day or night, in any activity you care to imagine, it is always possible to ponder any of these three signs, singularly or collectively, for there is nothing in the universe, whether it is your own mind and body or the furthest galaxy, that is outside these truths. It doesn't matter at all what your mood may be. View the world and all that is going on at the time, and bring one of these wonders to bear upon some element of that experience and ponder it.

Watch the change taking place in front of you, as nothing ever stays the same for long, and realize that everything is in a state of flux and can never ultimately be independent. And what happens when I think that this thing is somehow fixed and therefore graspable? Look outwards into the world in this way, but better still make it really personal and look inside yourself as well. Apply these three wonders to your body and mind as you move around. Look into mind and body through these characteristics without thinking. Look into your feelings and desires and aversions and emotions and passions in the same way – then use thinking to continue when thinking demands its place back. Any way you choose, let total anarchy reign! Just apply those three precious and profound tools to your every minute. These will familiarize you with the Dharma and take you back over and over again, with mindfulness, into yourself and into the present moment. More and more you will be able to stay with what you are doing. Try it. This is called 'skilful means for the chattering mind, and loss of awareness'.

It is the commitment to the energetic mental engagement of mindfulness in the moment that is the Dharma's most important tool. It is full of life, because it tempers and even stops the incessant karmic flow of thoughts that take us away from the experience of the fullness of life, and it is this lack of fullness (fulfilment) that is the root of dukkha. It is mindfulness that applies the brake and slows down the wheel of samsara, preparing the conditions for the diamond cutter of awareness to slice that samsaric wheel to shreds.

Awareness

Having looked at mindfulness we can now look at its best friend 'that which mindfulness is born of ': awareness. We humans not only have awareness, as all sentient beings must to one degree or another, we also possess the greatest jewel of all, self-awareness, that ability to know ourselves and, as it were, stand back and reflect on that knowing, which then gives us the ability to control and manipulate our actions. It is the highest evolution of awareness that sets us apart from all other forms of life, and when used to its highest potential it takes us straight as an arrow to Buddhahood.

What a wonderful aspect of our being to contemplate! When we really discover this mystery of mysteries on all its levels, it is the greatest of insights, one that when its ultimate understanding is revealed, is discovered to be the Buddha himself.

The whole of our Dharma practice is geared towards cultivating the habit of staying for as long as possible in that bare, naked awareness, where we know ourselves in every moment of being. To stay there for as long as our ability allows is truly to go beyond the world of samsara, because in those moments we are ceasing to create karma for ourselves and abiding in the still coolness that soon will take us to eternal freedom. The *Maha Satipatthana Sutta* states 'When you stand, know you are standing. When you sit, know you are sitting. When you walk, know you are walking. When you are lying down, know you are lying down'. But how do we manage to achieve this? We achieve this by cultivating the eightfold path.

The essence of the Path is to cultivate the ability to abide in the middle way, that state of being that develops over years of practice giving us the ability to engage in life to the full, but not to take hold of it and make it 'mine', nor to go the opposite way and turn away and reject life. Both are attachments, whichever way we want to react. These are the extremes of life. When we perfect letting go of these extremes we are no longer being pulled around by them, but rest in the cool of the middle – in the middle way. It is whilst in the cool of the middle that our self-awareness is at its brightest. It shines forth without the usual disturbances, and its innate ability to shine through the world and know its own reality is then at its peak.

We arrive at this profound state by cultivating our ethical behaviour and giving the heart peace, because it is harmonizing with its own natural goodness. From this stillness we can then strengthen our ability to concentrate and stay centred within our awareness. From this still cool centredness, our natural unspoilt awareness, we can use the insight tools of the Dharma (for example, the characteristics of impermanence, suffering, and not-self) that we have been skilfully and consistently nurturing to cut deeply into the created world of samsara. Liberation then comes from that still, cool state of awareness, and nowhere else.

Sometimes our awareness seems present for quite some time, and at other times we lose it altogether as our thoughts and mental pictures take over. In reality, awareness doesn't increase or decrease, it is consistent and ever present, but it is like the experience of the sun being covered by clouds, we may no longer see the sun but above the clouds it is still shining in perfection.

It is from awareness that the blinding world of thoughts and mental pictures is born but then obscures that very same awareness. The powerful forces that bring this world of opposites into being, that create the stage for those thoughts and impressions to play on, are also ultimately born of awareness. But that awareness, which is the receptacle of everything, is always cool and miraculously never touched by any of it. It doesn't need air to breathe nor food and water to live. Even at death, awareness does not die. At enlightenment, when the whole universe from heaven to hell, every realm of samsara that there is, dies and disappears, awareness doesn't; it is still there and not for a single moment is it ever touched or disturbed. Do you now begin to see how wonderful this awareness that we all have really is?

If through years of dedicated practice you manage to destroy the world of objects and still the unending flow of thoughts, you will be able to journey even deeper into the wonders of awareness – where does it go, where does it end, where is its source? You will be going deeper and deeper, going beyond the world, and beyond that pathetic self that wanted everything. Is this awareness then the real me? It must be. Are that sound over there and my awareness of it really two, or are they the same? If they are one then I am that sound, I am that bird, I am that mountain.

Awareness then isn't passive at all; ultimately it is anything but passive. Awareness finally discovers itself, and returns to itself. Awareness is everything, totality, all is one. One is only awareness and the great emptiness (shunyata) of love and knowledge, emptiness bathed in a warmth that loves all that is, that is infinite, full of bliss and eternally free – and is the real me.

Just stay with the awareness that reads the words on this page right now, just stay there and be still without falling back into mental chattering, and you will soon discover the truth behind these words you have just read. Truly, mindfulness and awareness could never be thought of as the same.

The Middle Way

Whatever part of the practice of the noble eightfold path we pursue, the goal is to one day attain a perfect balance between opposites. On the one side is grasping at our mental and physical experiences, and on the other reacting to them with a negative attitude of disinterest and rejection. The first is eternalism, because it is an act of trying to make something mine to keep, thus going against the natural law that everything is in a permanent state of change. The second is nihilism, not accepting the irresistible reality that we are part of life, and we can never remove ourselves from it, even with death.

This balance we call in Buddhism the middle way. As this is an area we are sometimes familiar with in our lives, we may feel we know enough about it, and not give it too much attention. Because we think it is easily understood we may put it to one side, believing there are other aspects of Dharma to study which are far more difficult to comprehend, and therefore must be more important than this doctrine of the middle way. But this is wrong.

I have tried to point to the practice in its various facets throughout this book, so I need not elaborate on any aspect of it just here. If the practitioner does not grasp at their ethical practice in their engagement with themselves, and others, and life in general, be it in word or actions, and say 'this is mine' – if they do not grasp at their developing concentration coming from their meditation and cultivation of mindfulness through their daily practice and say 'this is mine' – if they do not grasp at the wisdom that arises whilst using the tools of insight during practice and say, 'this is mine' – then a very profound state of mind will soon manifest. It is a state of mind that has never been known before, that is grounded in the perfection of wisdom of the ordinary mind. That ordinary mind, no longer driven by self-interest, becomes a creation of the wisdom of the middle way, as it no longer grasps at anything, but instead falls into equanimity towards all things. Equanimity means that the mind allows everything that comes to it to just arise and pass away, without reacting by grasping or rejecting. This is what you have been practising for all your Buddhist life. It is the perfection of practice, the perfection of the middle way, and the fulfilment of the fourth noble truth. When your mind reaches this exalted state and you do not slide back, enlightenment will very quickly come. That is absolutely guaranteed. The doctrine of the middle way may well be the simplest of doctrines, but it is also the most profound.

No Value Judgements

When we have committed ourselves to a daily sitting practice, some days we are concentrated while other days we are anything but. Concentration comes in varying degrees, and our lack of being able to concentrate comes in degrees as well, with our mind and feelings flowing first this way then that.

When concentration is good we may experience happiness or bliss that can permeate our whole being. At these times we couldn't be keener to sit. On other days we may go to our meditation with lots of negative feelings, thoughts, and emotions. Try as we might we simply can't put two seconds of concentration together, so that when we finish our meditation we often feel worse than when we started. This is because we assume that we have failed, and that the whole exercise was a waste of time. I am sure everyone reading this will have had these experiences from time to time, as we inevitably fall into value judgements, thinking either 'My meditation was good today' or 'My meditation was bad today'. But making those kinds of judgements is wrong, and really shows a lack of understanding of the Dharma and how it works. By all means say – if you must – 'I was concentrated today' or 'I wasn't concentrated today', because that is a simple statement of fact, but don't allow yourself to fall into those judgement traps.

I am personally convinced that if there is a wholehearted commitment, both sincere and deep, to the three jewels of Buddha, Dharma, Sangha – be it to the arising of the bodhicitta through the bodhisattva vows, or a commitment to the three jewels in a more traditional sense – something very profound takes place on a deep subconscious or even unconscious level. A message or signal is sent right into the heart of samsara – into its darkest, most unknown level – saying that you are no longer going to be the victim of this entrapment and bondage. This message is a statement that from this day forward you are going to work with wholehearted commitment to transform that darkness until you are free and liberated. In this way you set in motion an irreversible process that doesn't work from your consciousness down, but from your subconscious up. Because it is coming from this unknown depth you are never really in a position to know what is good and what is bad practice.

In your daily meditation practice, which is complementary and integral to an ongoing daily Dharma practice, avoid making the mistake of value judging. If you are cultivating the middle way and your practice is true, then try to recognize that it is really working much more on this subconscious level, and is beyond your ability to see and know directly. By determining to commit yourself to a consistent, balanced, daily practice, you are sending that clear and precise message deep into your psyche that the game is up. It is a message to those forces that you don't really understand, because at present they are largely unknown, that you are now determined to get to know and understand them. You are now prepared to open up to those forces that hitherto you have not been connected to, or have turned away from out of fear. You are committed to looking into them with understanding and embracing love should they arise from the subconscious. Through this process, in time, they will transform out of their present darkness.

It is your commitment to the practice, and to taking yourself to your meditation posture every day, that is the key to change. Even if you are sure it is a waste of time to sit today, still go to your cushion. Even if you were correct and you don't sit at all well, even if your mind is all over the place with not two seconds of concentration put together, still do it, understanding that what is important to change those dark forces is your consistent commitment to practice.

You will have a set time for your sitting, so stick to that. When you are feeling good about life go to your meditation and enjoy it, but stay with your set time. Don't decide to sit another five or ten minutes because you are concentrated. If you are feeling bad about life then go to your meditation and concentrate as best you can. Stay with your set time; don't decide to sit five or ten minutes less because you are struggling. By being consistent you are not judging your sitting – and because you are not in direct contact with your subconscious you are not qualified to judge anyway. Just stick to the form that you have taken on, and be as determined as you can in maintaining that consistency. It is no use judging good or bad, because we are not in a position to, nor is it our job to do so.

It is the determination to be consistent in all situations that sends repeated messages to those unfathomable depths of darkness that the game is up. That is the practice of the middle way, and it is the middle way that transforms our bondage to those forces of darkness and eternal becoming.

Change – Dharmic and Worldly

I have often been asked about the change that we all hope will come out of our practice, and how we can recognize it. We come to the practice hoping for change as well as for many other apparent reasons, but it is not a good idea to get too attached, becoming goal-oriented and wanting to turn into someone else, or even to have desires for enlightenment that we then carry around. It is natural enough to want to experience some sort of change: in ourselves, and in our relationships with others and the world. But although change does take place as we practise, it is invariably very difficult to identify and describe the changes that happen.

There are fundamentally two types of change, one worldly and the other Dharmic. An example of a worldly change would be something similar to an experience I went through whilst in my teens. I used to bite my nails habitually. It not only made my fingers look unsightly, it also encouraged my mother to keep going on at me! One day I decided that enough was enough, that I really must make the effort to break this habit. So I summoned up the conscious will and determination to focus on the habit of a lifetime, break it, and thus undertake some sort of change. For weeks, every time I went to put one of my fingers in my mouth I brought forth the will to resist the habit and temptation, until finally the desire and habit died. Change had come and I stopped. My mother was happy! 'David', she said 'well done, you have broken a habit of a lifetime!'

This was a deliberate, conscious act of will on my part. I worked to bring about change by focusing on a particular part of myself, working to stem the flow of an ingrained habit, until I could quite clearly see that it had been broken. That was a simple example, and I am sure most of us have made efforts down the years – especially at the turn of the year when we traditionally make a resolution to break an undesirable habit, so as to change for the better. But Dharmic change doesn't work like this.

If we have a true and consistent practice, we don't focus on a particular aspect of our personality at all, targeting it as something to change. Instead, we embrace and accept all of ourselves for what we are, without judging, in a spirit of openness. Thus we avoid the trap of focusing on particular aspects of our personality and wanting to change just those parts. This embracing of all that we are, opening up to and accepting it, is precisely the difference between a worldly pursuit and a Dharmic pursuit.

Opening up and accepting without reacting, in a consistent way, means being prepared to embark on a practice of giving up all the self-centred attachments that give us trouble. This needs to be done in a complete and uncompromising way, whilst engaging with life in a wholehearted and positive manner.

Unlike worldly change, which is often very obvious, such as my fingernail example, change brought about by Dharma practice will not be so easy to identify in a direct way. This is because the process of Dharmic change takes place right across the personality, not targeting any particular part of it. So it is the totality of ourselves that is being touched by that change.

Of course sometimes in our practice we may have to focus on a part of our personality that may rise to the surface. Because it is big and important, and interferes with the rest of the practice, we may have to work on it specifically. But this is not the general spirit of Dharma practice. That spirit is one of being open to all of ourselves with equanimity whilst engaging wholeheartedly with life.

Sometimes it is possible to get an inkling of how you have changed, such as when you react differently in a familiar situation from how you used to react in the past. You may, for example, find yourself meeting a person that you used to have all sorts of negative feelings towards – to the extent that you found it difficult to function comfortably around them. Then you encounter this person again after many years and see much the same person that you remember from all that time ago. Some time after this reunion you may suddenly realize how you now functioned very comfortably with them, and see that you must really have changed.

I think that is about as close as you can get to seeing change in an evident, direct way. Worldly change is something conscious and obvious, and invariably about one thing, but Dharmic change actually takes place on a subconscious or even unconscious level. Because it 'spreads itself' across our being it becomes almost impossible to pinpoint and identify. Being very subtle, it cannot be known in the ordinary direct way.

I remember very well that when I first started to practise Zen I had two lists in my mind. One contained all the things that I didn't like about myself that I wanted to get rid of, and the other was a list of all the virtues and characteristics of a good man that I wanted to develop. I thought 'Right, I'll start at the top of the list and work through each one I don't like, then tick them off. Then I'll cultivate all the desirable things here on the second list, and tick them off one by one, so that I end up being the person that I've always wanted to be.' I soon learned to forget that approach, as it became clear to me that the practice and the change it produced didn't work in such a clear, obvious, (and self-centred) way. I learned to let go of those desires, and to accept myself just the way I was. I would suggest that you develop the same attitude towards your natural and understandable desire for change. Real change is beyond the self's ability to know, because it is that very experience of self that is changed through Dharma practice.

Change, in the real Dharmic sense, is actually nothing to do with us. It is a slow taming and transforming of our life-energy. This energy is bound up and deluded by attachments, which are themselves created and driven by the sense of self and ego that possesses and shapes our personality. When real Dharmic change takes place, this life-energy transforms back into its original nature on a deep subconscious level. In our original nature, there is no desire for change.

Karma and Rebirth

The whole subject of karma and rebirth is one of the great fascinations and sources of wonderment in Buddhism. It attracts attention possibly as much as any facet of the teachings, but what good is it to us in our everyday practice? I once asked my teacher in Sri Lanka something on this subject. His reply was 'Theory, it's all just theory.' I don't expect for one moment that he doubted the doctrine. Most Easterners wouldn't even question it. What he meant was that there was little use from the point of view of concrete, everyday practice in getting caught up in the imagery that has been created on this subject largely by the Indian mind.

I was once asked at a book launch what I thought about this endless cycle of coming and going through endless lives. Personally I have always thought that the best way to use this teaching was as a spur to greater efforts in the practice, so that one day the karmic propensities that create form – and yet another life – are transformed, thus breaking this eternal cycle of rebirth and suffering.

When I first came to Buddhism and Zen this was not a subject I was ever encouraged to investigate and study. In fact it was one of those taboo subjects that no one would bring up. Now, looking back, I feel this was an error, for to get some sort of grasp of the law of karma and its implications, including rebirth, is very helpful for practice. As with many other aspects of the teaching and philosophy of Buddhism, when investigating karma we must be careful not to get caught up with the imagery it creates. Rather we need to reflect on the doctrine and take it on board lightly, allowing ourselves to create a more objective overall picture of samsara that helps form the background to our practice.

Like many people in the West I was brought up a Christian – a Roman Catholic actually. One of the aspects of Christianity that always gave me trouble was the idea that life was somehow just a one-off experience that you had to get right, or you would end up in hell for all eternity. I just couldn't equate that teaching with the obvious inequalities of opportunity to go to Heaven that are presented to us at birth, both physically and mentally. Had God really created us, with all the inequalities that I could see all around me? Contemplating this, the only conclusion I could ever come to was that if he had done so he must surely be very twisted.

But when I came across the law of karma it made instant sense to me. Once I discovered that we are actually the creators and heirs to our actions, that we have to live out their consequences through an endless series of lives, it immediately answered my questions about the inequality and lopsidedness of life. This realization was very important for me. It allowed me to embrace and settle into the practice, because it presented an acceptable picture of the nature and reality of life.

All religions have a fear element within their doctrine – some more than others – and the fear element in Buddhism is the doctrine of the endless suffering and lottery of rebirth. Just to contemplate the consequences of this reality should be all the spur we need to commit ourselves to serious practice in order to get ourselves out of that endless cycle of birth, death, and suffering.

When I was in robes in Sri Lanka, during a period when insight was flowing very deeply, I was contemplating this very subject one day whilst relaxing in my hut. Without any warning, over a period of a few seconds every life that I have lived, and clear seeing of the reality of all those lives, arose within me. As every life came up and passed through the transcendental mind's eye, the reality of the beginning, middle, and end of every one of those lives was seen. (There was never a seeing of any details of the lives, for this is not of interest to the transcendental mind. Details of past lives would be the domain of the ordinary mind that has perfected the dhyanas – a practice that has never interested me because it has only worldly fruits and is devoid of true wisdom.) But the number of lives seen was quite ungraspable. There was never a definable beginning to the start of the cycle of becoming, with the number of lives going beyond the capacity of even the transcendental mind's ability to comprehend. This had a very strong impact on me. It made me sit down and contemplate this whole business of birth and death.

I do not consider myself to be a negative person with a negative view of life, but for some hours I allowed myself to sit and contemplate that aspect. I contemplated the negative, the suffering, the fear, and left to one side for the time being the paradox of the wonder and miracle of life of which we all partake. It is a topic that we all could turn ourselves towards and muse over from time to time.

I came into this life experiencing the pain of birth, and have spent most of my life trying as best I can to avoid any more of it. I could see fear as suffering's constant companion. There is fear of life's general suffering, but also specifically fear of loneliness, loss, and death, which is a much deeper fear, and a deeper sense of suffering. I have always pursued happiness in the hope of avoiding suffering. I have sought contentment in the hope that I would never have to face fear – but somehow I have never quite pulled it off. Sometimes I have tasted happiness and contentment, but often in those precious moments I have recognized that it would soon begin to slip through my fingers, and I would have to start all over again.

I have spent a lifetime pursuing this goal of contentment, whether consciously or unconsciously, with the frustration of knowing that ultimately I am never going to achieve it. This pursuit will no doubt last throughout my years. On top of that, during that pursuit I will have to try not to be preoccupied, but rather to accept that this body at any moment could give me pain and serious trouble.

It was not difficult to see that this body makes me live my life at its constant beck and call. It requires food and water, and general attention. However inconvenient this attention may be at times, the body still demands priority over everything. I can see that, however wonderful a machine it may be, I am still restricted by its demands.

Yet ironically, despite the resentment that sometimes can come towards this compulsory engagement, there is still a curious and very powerful attachment to it, even though I am aware that could at any moment it let me down.

It will not seek my permission to die and go into change. It will not apologize if I happen to be in the middle of something important. It will just do it. In that dying there will inevitably be pain, and I will be then be faced with its closest friend – fear. The dreaded fear of death will finally have arrived. All of my life I have conveniently avoided thinking of this day, but now the one guarantee in life has finally come. Along with it come the fear, the experience of suffering, and the fear of the unknown that follows. Whilst in my life I have always chased the light, now the darkness comes, the darkness which is the one guarantee in life. And just how many times have I had this experience of death?

If you would like to get to grips with the number of lives you must surely have lived, you can embark on a little exercise that will bring home to you the endless cycle of rebirth and suffering that we all seem willing to partake in. Think of the number one. Now double it, then double the result of that sum. Double it again, and so on. Of course you have things to do in your life, so you can't be doing these sums all the time. Nevertheless whenever you think of it, in times of boredom or whenever it's convenient, continue doubling the total. Soon you will need a piece of paper to keep track, and soon after that a calculator. As the number gets ever larger you will require a computer. Pursue this exercise at your leisure, right through your life, and when the time finally arrives to leave the body that can no longer support you, just check on the figure that you are currently at. When you run your eyes along that number, which will be way beyond your ability to grasp, realize that that number just scratches the surface of the number of times you have experienced the phenomenon of death that you are now about to go through yet again.

Maybe at that time you will regret not making the effort to put an end to this hideous cycle that you have no control over. Maybe you will think that if only you had made the effort while you were well, you might have come to this point with a smile on your face, in the knowledge that this was the last time. The judge of death, Yama – whom you have encountered countless times in the past – will come to you yet again as he has done every time at your death, with his piercing eyes and hideous laugh. He then will grab you by the scruff of your neck and drag you into another life, whether you like it or not, to perpetuate this endless cycle. At that moment it may dawn on you that you could have brought this cycle to an end. The people you have had faith in, the Buddha, your teacher, all the wise men and women throughout the history of Buddhism, told you that going beyond birth and death could be achieved. If only you had pursued the Path to take you out of this cycle.... Then, instead of Yama coming and roaring with laughter and enjoying his power over you, you could have greeted him with a warm and loving smile. You could have drawn the sword of wisdom that you had created, a sword honed to a fine sharpness by a lifetime of dedicated practice, and cut him in two.

Whilst contemplating these negative realities of life, I realized what good karma I had. Not only had I come to human birth where liberation from the wheel is possible, I had also had the good karma to be born in a time when the Dharma still exists, and what is more, the good karma to hear that Law. These thoughts made me resolve that I was never going to give up this practice while I had the good karma to continue. I am determined that it will be me and not Yama who will be smiling the next time we meet.

Self

One of the most fascinating aspects of Dharma training is working to understand the subject of the self. This really is the great mystery. If we observe ourselves, and the motivations, fears, desires, etc. that seem to take hold of our lives most of the time, we see that just about every mental movement we make seems to come from the conviction that there is a fixed person somewhere inside our mind and even inside our body. This sense of self, ego, or me, seems to pervade our whole consciousness, yet Buddhism will always deny its very existence! There doesn't appear to be another religion or spiritual path that makes such a statement. Even if you were to study the metaphysics of the abhidharma, a study that leaves no stone unturned in dissecting the human condition and its experience, or to study the many commentaries and teachings of schools and masters, they, and Buddhism in general, will nowhere affirm this experience all of us are apparently having most of the time.

Even the second of the four noble truths doesn't state that the cause of suffering is the self. It says that it is desire that is the cause of suffering. But what is it that is desiring? What is this self that doesn't exist?

The experience of self always takes place in a state of duality. The sense of duality, of me here and the world out there, is the normal state of being for us all. This experience of separateness allows that state of individuality to arise, and it is whilst in that state of individuality that the self will manifest.

Thoughts will come from that state of individuality and a self-identity will arise. Those thoughts that were neutral in their original state then become 'me and mine', and out of that the world and the world of self-volition come into being. The strength of being that comes from a sense of self is so great that it even remains for quite some time after those thoughts stop. The whole phenomenon of self and ego relies on duality in order to come into being. So when the conditions are not there for it, the self is not subdued, nor does it go into hiding; it quite literally does not exist.

If you dedicate your meditation for a hundred years to the search for the self you will never find it, yet it possesses us throughout our day. It is this mystery beyond all mysteries that we so often investigate with the wonderful tools used in insight meditation. We understand that it is this very sense of self that gathers up consciousness and being, and creates this delusion of 'This is me, this is mine' that we are then ensnared by.

The nearest I have ever come to describing this sense of a self to myself is that it is as if I've entered a room full of furniture and many, many things, and the air is filled with a perfume. I then undertake the task of trying to find the source of this perfume. I begin to search. Wherever I investigate I only experience the smell. It is everywhere. It is on all the furniture and on all the objects I investigate. Everything is saturated by the smell, yet I can never find its source or any tangible centre from which it comes. This seems to be similar to any search for the self that I've ever embarked on. It can never be found in and of itself, as it will always need an object, whether mental or physical, in order to arise. Take away the object and you take away the self. And it is because of the self or ego's non-existence that we should not take this delusion too seriously.

The self is not a thing in itself but a phenomenon that arises due to circumstances. When the circumstances are not present the self is quite literally non-existent. We talk sometimes of reincarnation, but that implies a self or person or some sense of identity that travels to another birth, so it would actually be more accurate to describe it as rebirth, as this is less likely to suggest some sort of self-identity doing the travelling. It is a set of conditions that does not die but abides mysteriously deep within us that does this travelling, and is mysteriously stored beyond all forms of knowing and consciousness. It is vast amounts of karmic seeds created by past actions that do the migrating – until they find suitable conditions to germinate and take a new birth. When those seedlings ripen, unless we understand their nature, the conditions are produced for a sense of self to arise once more.

When we come to the practice of the Buddha-Dharma, we may approach it from any number of perspectives, but ultimately these various ways are all designed to help us to see the reality of our being, and thus free ourselves from the bondage of non-understanding. At no time in our search for truth are we advised to get involved with this self. On the contrary, we are encouraged to turn away from it, and to cultivate the reality that reveals itself when we are not caught up and blinded by it.

This delusion of a self-identity and the massive burden it creates may not be something that needs to be high-lighted so much for Easterners. In the East people don't generally carry around a burden of self, and the guilt that characterizes it, to anything like the degree we Western people do. This burden that we Westerners carry, which is frequently the source of our difficulty in undertaking this practice, is unique in the history of Buddhism. West-ern culture typically emphasizes the importance of the individual, and the virtue of striving for yourself in life rather than negating yourself for the greater good. It is this tendency that creates this perceived need for a strong, assertive, successful self or ego.

This strong and 'unhealthy' sense of self that we West-erners have becomes a source of negativity that makes us dislike, or even hate, ourselves. We may view ourselves as useless and no good, and see ourselves in generally unwholesome terms. Then this self of ours becomes the unbearably heavy burden that many of us experience. This burden can become so massive that it prevents us from engaging in any meaningful practice at all. We get stuck and weighed down with it as it takes us over more and more.

I feel strongly about this subject, and need to air it, because I had a strong focus on the self in my early training and found it to be thoroughly unhelpful and indeed oppressive. It just pandered to the negativity I was already carrying around with me anyway. I reached a point where guilt almost took over, as I began to see everything I did as a self-centred act – all 'I' – that by definition made me feel useless, and was sinful and wrong and outside of practice. The burden of self seemed at times to be actually increasing rather than decreasing. There was such an emphasis and focus on this 'I' that I almost became convinced that it was the sixth skandha! This is not the way of the Dharma.

Dharmachari Vessantara writes of the Western preoccupation with the self in his excellent book *Meeting the Buddhas* (p. 142) and leaves little further to add on this predominantly Western phenomenon:

> Buddhism teaches that to gain Enlightenment we have to go beyond, or see through, the fixed unchanging ego, with its aversions and predilections. Unfortunately this sometimes leads people to take cudgels to themselves. In their attempts to stamp out the ego, they bring themselves to a virtual standstill. Sometimes they become so suspicious of themselves, constantly spying on themselves for signs of ego, that they become negatively self-obsessed, and fail to make any real spiritual progress.

Dharma practice is not exactly to turn away from this self and ignore it, but rather to turn away from it while retaining a watchful eye, as your understanding of reality deepens. Don't feel guilty when you make a mistake and see it as all 'I' – the great sin of Buddhism – and make a problem out of it. If you do, you are playing the self's game. Instead, acknowledge it and accept it as a part of you that you need to make friends with. Dharma practice is ultimately only about making friends with yourself. Open to that mental and physical passionate drive of attachment that is driven by the sense of self, and contain it. Containing it is to not give in to it; not to give in to it is to acknowledge its non-existence.

Spirituality and Faith

I have intentionally left till last this reflection on spirituality and its nature, as I consider it to be the most important aspect of our training. If we choose to ignore this
aspect, and do not make it central to our practice, I'm
convinced that it will not be possible to mature our
understanding to any deep degree. To ignore the innate
spirituality of practice is to ignore the heart, and unless
the heart is fully engaged with the whole of our practice,
it will never truly open. If we decide to pursue a 'non
spiritual' attitude, the natural warmth and wisdom of the
heart will not fully open and express itself. If that is the
case then the true wonder and mystery of this miracle
that we all partake of every day will never truly reveal
itself. But what needs to be known for there to be a
spiritual practice? I would say there are two aspects that
characterize spiritual practice.

Ethics is intentionally nurturing wholesome skilful
means, so this is always ongoing in our wholehearted
engagement with daily life. Ethics also implies bringing
forth restraint, so if a habit is seen to be unwholesome
and unskilful, even harmful, either to yourself or to
others, then efforts should be made to avoid getting
caught and carried away by that attachment. This, of
course, is fine, but there is an inherent danger in making
these judgements, of becoming judgemental and one-
sided, so we must be ever watchful to guard against that
tendency. If we want to nurture true spiritual practice that
leads to complete understanding of the Dharma, we need

to engage with the whole of ourselves. This means expanding on the common basic ethical framework, and trying to address all our attachments – whether we see them as unwholesome or not, and including attachment to our views – with a spirit of inclusivity.

The first aspect, therefore, is to cultivate the attitude of giving up attachment to the whole of one's self, not a practice whereby we say, 'I will give up attachment to this because it is unwholesome and negative' but 'I will keep hold of this because it is wholesome and positive.' If you go down this road there is a danger of developing the ego still further, but now with spiritual conceit, as you attach yourself to what you consider good and bad. Eventually this may lead you to become split, in an opinionated and judgemental state which breeds intolerance and bigotry. It is the attitude of willingly giving up all attachment that sets Dharma practice apart from other forms of self-help that are so prevalent in the West these days. If we decide to take on some sort of therapy or psychoanalytical activity that we think will cure our problems, this is a different approach to spirituality.

In therapy we tend to target a particular aspect of our make-up that we want to change, so we focus on that part and work on it, usually with someone else, and try to get to the bottom of the problem and then do something about it. We extract the problem from the whole, or at least most of it, in order to deal with it. Many, many people come to the Dharma because they have problems they would like to resolve, but the way we deal with these perceived problems within Dharma practice is not to segregate them and work on them individually but to include them in the whole practice. Dharma practice is not about picking and choosing, it is about opening up to the whole of ourselves, saying 'yes' to everything there, and cultivating Dharmic skills to transform what we have found.

It is the willingness to open to ourselves that for most of us is a revolutionary, indeed frightening, act. However, we learn through our developing understanding of practice that this is the correct way of transformation. Our willingness to accept and contain all of ourselves with a spirit of openness is the very essence of spirituality. This involves resisting those familiar attachments: our wants and aversions, and our endless views and opinions.

It is the willingness to give oneself up in totality that transforms the endless cycle of becoming that we have all been bound to since time began, and it is only the willingness to surrender ourselves in totality that will put an end to that cycle. This must not be misunderstood as a negation of life; far from it. Our practice is to engage fully and wholeheartedly with life, in a skilful way that does not promote the neurotic attachments that we all have anyway. We need to nurture a warm heart, as a replacement for those long-held habits that caused us the troubles that brought us to the practice of the Buddha-Dharma in the first place. But what should we be surrendering ourselves to?

When we come to Buddhism, read about it, and listen to those who talk about it, we learn about the Buddha's life, and the struggles that he went through until finally he discovered the truth. We read and listen as his teachings and the philosophy of life that Buddhism offers are explained to us, those precise teachings that have led men and women out of suffering for many hundreds of years. Through this a spark is struck within. We recognize that what we are now learning feels right and makes good sense, and is what we've been searching for, whether consciously or unconsciously, for a long time. I don't believe when this happens it is at all an intellectual reaction; it is an intuitive experience that we feel compelled to investigate. We may read more, or we may straight away take up a Dharma practice, but there is something there that feels right that keeps us moving forward, and that I would suggest is the second aspect of spirituality – faith.

Faith arises in the Buddha and in his teachings. Faith is not intellectual but a feeling, it is a feeling that what you are now learning is right. You don't yet have any direct experience to confirm that feeling, but somehow you know it is right, and you are prepared to trust it and allow it to carry you forward. This trust that comes from inner faith will deepen as true practice deepens.

Focus on the place where trust and faith is centred, where the Buddha and Dharma is, and you will discover that it is precisely where your heart is. There is no 'logic' here. There are no systems or methods either, but it is where all the paradoxes that arise within your practice are peacefully settled. The daily practice that you are becoming more and more familiar with should have this centre as a part of it, and it is to this centre that we learn to surrender. Dharma practice is about gathering up and containing all of ourselves, with a willingness to bear with all those habitual reactions that we are no longer prepared to play along with. Gather all of those likes and dislikes, wants and aversions, that are fired by the passionate emotional drive of 'me', and offer them back into the faith and trust with which you are now becoming familiar and intimate. Unburden yourself and give all of it, without reservation and conditions, back into the great mystery that lies within each of us.

Something that has been at the centre of my practice down the years has been the daily cultivation of bowing. This symbolizes for me what the whole of Dharma practice is about. In those precious moments of kneeling and touching my forehead to the ground I will gather up in my mind the whole of myself, not just 'David' and all the views and opinions that he is attached to, but also all the wonderful Dharma understanding that has revealed itself down the years. I gather it all up, and finally, including the gatherer, hand it all back to the Buddha – not the Buddha that is out there in that rupa in front of me, but the Buddha that lies deep within. I always bow three times. On the first bow I quietly ask the Buddha to forgive me. Maybe to forgive a recent experience that I've felt I had been unskilful in. I ask the Buddha to forgive all the views and attachments that I cherish that have brought such suffering, not just to myself but to so many in the world, that not only cause harm, but keep me fearful and separate from the wonder of life. On the second bow I ask for help in the task of surrendering 'David' and his continual drive to possess what he wants and control all that comes to threaten him – for the strength of self-will is indeed great, and too powerful for me to work with on my own. On the third bow I ask to be accepted back into the eternal mystery that is beyond time and the suffering of life and death, and this imprisonment to self.

The three bows contain my deepest commitment to faith. Down the years that faith has at times been so strong that it has broken the barrier of separateness between the Buddha and me, and my requests for support – usually in times of great distress – have been heard. Do not misunderstand me. I am not saying I have faith in a god or some power 'out there' and separate from me. In those times of communion it is revealed that all along it has been myself that has caused this separation from all that is. It has just been my own foolish mind at play. So in truth I am not separate at all, and indeed have never been. In these times of communion the deepest commitment to going for refuge is fulfilled, for true going for refuge is to go beyond suffering, to be truly free, to return to the warmth of the human heart, and the home that you never left.

BY THE SAME AUTHOR

A RECORD OF AWAKENING
*The rare and inspiring example of a life consistently and
uncompromisingly dedicated to the practice of the Dharma.*
Urgyen Sangharakshita

The remarkable fruit of more than twenty years immersion in
Buddhist practice: a practice that has been both deep and
far-reaching.

In this book David Smith, 'an ordinary working-class chap'
who came across Buddhism, shares his extraordinary inner
experience. Taking us through his journey from initial practice
in the Zen tradition and three years as a Theravadin monk to
his recent years as a lay practitioner in East London he describes
the basic principles of his practice and the process whereby the
'tap root of ignorance' is cut and the Awakened Mind is born.
His account reminds us that the Awakened Mind is within the
reach of every one of us prepared to make the effort.

152 pages
ISBN 0 9542475 1 5
£7.99

AVAILABLE FROM ALOKA PUBLICATIONS

www.dharmamind.net
information@dharmamind.net